Young Irelander Abroad
The Diary of Charles Hart

IRISH NARRATIVES

IRISH NARRATIVES
Series edited by David Fitzpatrick

Personal narratives of past lives are essential for understanding any field of history. They provide unrivalled insight into the day-to-day consequences of political, social, economic or cultural relationships. Memoirs, diaries and personal letters, whether by public figures or obscure witnesses of historical events, will often captivate the general reader as well as engrossing the specialist. Yet the vast majority of such narratives are preserved only among the manuscripts or rarities in libraries and archives scattered over the globe. The aim of this series of brief yet scholarly editions is to make available a wide range of narratives concerning Ireland and the Irish over the last four centuries. All documents, or sets of documents, are edited and introduced by specialist scholars, who guide the reader through the world in which the text was created. The chosen texts are faithfully transcribed, the biographical and local background explored, and the documents set in historical context. This series will prove invaluable for university and school teachers, providing superb material for essays and textual analysis in class. Above all, it offers a novel opportunity for readers interested in Irish history to discover fresh and exciting sources of personal testimony

David Fitzpatrick teaches history at Trinity College, Dublin. His books include *Politics and Irish Life, 1913–1921* (1977, reissued 1998), *Oceans of Consolation: Personal Accounts of Irish Migration to Australia* (1995) and *The Two Irelands, 1912–1939* (1998).

For a full list of titles in the *Irish Narratives* series see inside front cover.

Young Irelander Abroad
The Diary of Charles Hart

Edited by
Brendan Ó Cathaoir

CORK UNIVERSITY PRESS

First published in 2003 by
Cork University Press
Crawford Business Park
Crosses Green
Cork
Ireland

British Library Cataloguing in Publication Data
A CIP catalogue record for this book is available from the British Library.
ISBN 1 85918 360 3
A CIP record for this book is available from the Library of Congress.

Typesetting by Red Barn Publishing, Skeagh, Skibbereen, Co. Cork
Printed in Ireland by ColourBooks, Baldoyle, Co. Dublin

www.corkuniversitypress.com

Contents

Acknowledgements

This attempt to turn darkness into light would not have been under-taken without Professor Myles Dillon's typescript of his grand-uncle's diary. The copy, while containing numerous inaccuracies, was an indispensable requisite. Deciphering Charles Hart's handwriting unaided would have proved a daunting task. Dillon hoped to publish the Hart Diary in *Irish Historical Studies*. Professor T. Desmond Williams replied that, 'while it is a valuable historical document, it is not quite the kind of thing which we could publish. . . It is also rather long . . .' (letter dated 20 February 1962 found with the diary typescript, MS 6906, Dillon Papers, Trinity College, Dublin). One could add that this manuscript required extensive editing and explanation.

Professor John M. Dillon provided, besides much encouragement, a picture of his great grand-uncle (taken in New York by the renowned photographer, Mathew Brady). Professor David Fitzpatrick gave valuable editorial guidance. Dr C. J. Woods helped with annotations. Stuart Ó Seanóir, of the TCD Manuscripts Room, assisted with Hart's hieroglyphic handwriting. I wish to thank the Board of Trinity College for permission to publish this document. I am indebted to many others including: the staff and archivists of the National Library of Ireland and of the Royal Irish Academy; Professor James Dunkerley, Institute of Latin American Studies, University of London; my *Irish Times* colleague, Deaglán de Bréadún; Nina Nazionale and Roane Carey, New York Historical Society; the late Patrick O'Donoghue, CM, Castle-knock College, Dublin; Professor Máirtín Ó Murchú, School of Celtic Studies, Dublin Institute for Advanced Studies; and my wife and fellow historian, Eva Ó Cathaoir. Finally, my nephew Michael F. Cahir and daughter Katharina provided essential computer assistance.

Introduction

Charles Hart lacked consistency. In 1848 he expected the famished people to fight, while he went to the United States to avoid possible arrest. He wrote in his diary that it was man's lot to labour, but during his year in New York he was a gentleman, albeit a studious one, of leisure, whose circumscribed middle-class existence separated him from the harrowing lives of the Famine refugees. On arrival in that city he took a room in the Astor Hotel, whereas they streamed into ghettos like the Five Points intersection, which, according to Bishop John Hughes, contained 'the poorest and most wretched population in the world — the scattered debris of the Irish nation'.[1] In 1848, some 91,000 disembarked; by 1855, the number of Irish-born had risen to 175,000, representing 28 per cent of the population of New York, now containing almost as many Irish people as Dublin.[2] Experiencing none of the sting of discrimination, Hart was a Victorian polymath, a semi-politically-engaged intellectual incapable of violence, whose bedtime reading included trigonometry and theology.

Charles Henry Hart was born on 4 November 1824 in Blackhall Street, Dublin. He would be the last of the Harts of Greenogue, a family with United Irish links. His father, William Francis Hart, was a solicitor whose firm, Hart and O'Hara, became one of the first Catholic law partnerships to begin practice after the relaxation of the penal laws.[3] Hart attended Castleknock College, Dublin, in 1836–8, and St Mary's, Oscott.[4] His comments on education suggest he was not happy at boarding schools. When Charles's father died in 1831 his mother, Christiana Teresa, moved with the three surviving children to the home of her brother, William O'Hara, at Druid Lodge, Killiney, County Dublin. In 1847 his sister, Adelaide, married John Blake Dillon, who had founded the *Nation* newspaper with Thomas Davis and Charles Gavan Duffy.[5]

Hart was a minor Young Irelander, in the shadow of his brother-in-law. He flirted briefly with militant nationalism during the year of revolutions in Europe. The sudden collapse of established regimes in the spring of

1848 led Irish nationalists to believe that repeal of the Union could be achieved with similar ease. The Paris revolution, in particular, gave new hope to the divided and dispirited repeal movement. However, the trial and conviction of John Mitchel in May injected a note of realism into Young Ireland calculations. Mitchel was sentenced to fourteen years' transportation under the new Treason Felony Act. The Irish Confederation, established after the split with O'Connell, began to organise clubs which could form the nucleus of a national guard. Mitchel's young brother, William, and a solicitor, Martin O'Flaherty, were sent as agents to the US.[6] Hart would join them shortly.

Nevertheless, his involvement in the half-hearted conspiracy was slight. He had canvassed in Waterford when Thomas Francis Meagher attempted to win a parliamentary seat. During Mitchel's trial, he sat on the platform at a protest meeting against jury packing chaired by Dillon. Meagher encountered Hart with Dillon in a covered vehicle in Merrion Square on 22 July, reports having reached Dublin that *habeas corpus* was to be suspended in Ireland.[7] Dillon and Meagher persuaded William Smith O'Brien, MP, to lead a premature revolt, which ended in County Tipperary one week later in ignominious failure.

Hart left home the day Dublin Castle issued a proclamation offering rewards of £300 for the capture of Dillon, Meagher and Michael Doheny. Dillon wrote from a hiding place in the west that 'Charles and Mr O'Hara had gone somewhere avoiding an arrest'. Although Hart did not feature in the *Hue and Cry*, which carried unflattering descriptions of the leaders, perhaps he was prudent to leave before police raided Druid Lodge searching for his brother-in-law.[8] The cunning O'Hara influenced the private counsels of the Young Ireland party. He had overreached himself, a correspondent wrote to Duffy, already detained in Newgate Prison, 'for his connection with Dillon will damage him as much as if he had been personally concerned in the affair'. When Dillon escaped to New York, however, O'Hara — returning from France after the crisis had blown over — assured his sister that the family 'are rising rather than sinking'.[9]

Hart's diary opens with his departure from Druid Lodge on 28 July

1848, but he did not begin writing it until he reached New York. The diary continues, with major time gaps, until Hart's return to Dublin more than a year later. He wrote in a foreword: 'I have determined to note down anything I can remember of the voyage over and of my thoughts and feelings, as I have often regretted not having kept some record during former travels.' He added modestly: 'Tho' these things may not be in any degree interesting to others, they can hardly fail to be highly so to oneself. If naturally and truly written they may also be very instructive.'

His boyish delight in travel is spiced with a whiff of conspiracy. On the way to Dalkey station he tore a recipe for making gunpowder from his pocket book. Hart imagined he was being shadowed by a detective as he bought a ticket to travel by the atmospheric railway to Kingstown [Dún Laoghaire]. In Liverpool he marched 'about five miles to the Railway Hotel to mislead the enemy, a porter carrying my trunk before me'. This was *opéra bouffe* — except for the unfortunate porter — but at the time neither Hart nor the authorities realized the insurrection had been a fiasco.

His diary contains vivid impressions of American life. Acute observation is interspersed with the banal. An ardent admirer of the young republic, he inspected sites associated with the War of Independence (1775–83) and West Point military academy. Hart and his friends walked extensively in New York and its environs, took two trips up the Hudson River — then a fashionable excursion for the educated bourgeoisie — and visited places identified in Washington Irving's story, *The Legend of Sleepy Hollow*, which had been read to him at Castleknock. He attended the inauguration of Zachary Taylor as twelfth US president. Understandably, the young Irishman lacked the vision of Thoreau, who said Americans 'must cease to hold slaves, and to make war on Mexico, though it cost them their existence as a people'.[10] Hart's remarks about African Americans are perceptive, if patronising. He found the slaves encountered in Washington, DC, 'less intellectual looking than the free blacks of New York'.

He was regaled by newly-arrived émigrés with accounts of the Ballingarry affray, which Doheny referred to as 'Mr O'Brien's disaster'.[11]

They are important not for the accuracy of the information imparted —
although the reported sympathy shown by some magistrates and policemen towards Meagher and O'Brien is of interest — but for the insight
offered into the Young Ireland mind. For instance, in the one distasteful
passage in the diary, Hart infers with approval that O'Brien had been pre-
pared to sacrifice the Widow McCormack's children for 'the chance of
striking a blow', by smoking out the constabulary sheltering in her house.
This story is as unlikely as the claim made at the subsequent trial that,
when the police refused to surrender, O'Brien said: 'Slash away, boys,
and slaughter the whole of them.' His brother Robert reported he was
'much delighted' to be relieved of that charge.[12] His latest biographer
concludes that, if O'Brien had been deterred from burning the house 'by
the thought of sacrificing five small children, this meant he was a decent
human being but an ineffectual rebel'.[13]

Terence Bellew MacManus, who led the attack on the 'warhouse',
was ordered to desist by O'Brien, who thought the widow had been
sent round 'by the police to say they will make terms'.[14] One of Hart's
informants, John Kavanagh, who was wounded at Ballingarry and
escaped via France to the US, recorded hearing O'Brien say to the constabulary: 'I want you to give up your arms, we shall not hurt a man of
you, you are Irishmen.' Kavanagh saw policemen shake his hand.[15]
During this parley stone-throwing began and the police replied with
their carbines, killing two insurgents and wounding others.[16]

The sagacious William Joseph O'Neill Daunt wrote in his journal:

> Disastrous news of Smith O'Brien. I had prayed him to avoid all col-
> lision with the law, advice which he has unhappily disregarded. It
> seems that he has engaged in a driftless and unaccountable affray with
> the police, and is now hiding among the mountains of Tipperary with
> a government reward of £500 upon his head. How men will throw
> themselves away! Of what avail is Smith O'Brien henceforth to our
> [repeal] cause? One rash act destroys his utility. My heart bleeds for
> him. I have intense confidence in his honour and in his devotion to Ire-
> land. . . How completely is the wisdom of O'Connell's moral force
> agitation justified by all this wild trashery of pike and rifle and military

clubbing. The *émeute*, too, occurred under circumstances that gave the maximum of disadvantage to the insurgents, and which were calculated to disparage unfairly the physical power of the people. It is scarcely possible to conceive a more complete mistake. The government have arrested most of the leaders of the pike and rifle agitation. They have thus probably averted much bloodshed. The opposite policy of fomenting the insurrection and producing the explosion was practised by the blood-thirsty government of 1797–8.[17]

O'Brien, MacManus, Meagher and Patrick O'Donohue were convicted of high treason and sentenced to be hanged. As the affair had been such a humiliating fiasco, the British government had no intention of enforcing the death penalty. The sentences were commuted to transportation for life. MacManus, in a narrative written before his arrest and conveyed to Duffy in Newgate in August 1848, asserted that those implicated were the 'precursors of Irish Independence'.[18]

Dillon and Hart revered the quixotic O'Brien, whose decision to take the field owed more to ideas of duty and honour than to any realistic assessment of the situation. In New York they avoided the factions which grew up around the 'discomfited revolutionists', while disapproving of Doheny and Thomas D'Arcy McGee. McGee, who had started a New York edition of the *Nation*, persisted in criticizing O'Brien's leadership. Furthermore, Dillon considered him an opportunist, who lacked 'good feeling . . . has been puffing and publishing himself . . . is trading upon the misfortunes of his country and his friends'. Doheny, the fastidious Dillon reported to his wife, 'spends his evenings in a public house, reciting to an audience of "*rowdies*" his exploits and his hair-breath escapes'.[19] Hart objected to Doheny's 'unhandsome and false insinuations and statements about SO'B'. Unlike Hart, Doheny had endured privations during his flight from Ireland. He spent the rain-sodden autumn of 1848 wandering in Munster with James Stephens, the future Fenian leader. On arrival in New York he lost no time in writing an account of his adventures. *The Felon's Track* achieved popularity with generations of Irish people following its publication in 1849. He dedicated it to James Shields, an Irish-American general, whom the characteristically ineffectual Hart failed to see at a presidential levee.

Horace Greeley, founder-editor of the *New York Tribune* and friend of nationalist Ireland, suggested that a public meeting be held to welcome the 'ten or twelve patriotic young Irishmen who were engaged in the recent movement for Ireland's emancipation. Some of them have come with a price upon their heads.' Hart's associates thought events in Ireland merited a dignified silence, and said so in letters to the *Tribune*. William Mitchel wrote: 'I have a strong aversion to see the miserable burlesque of '48 again raised up as a spectacle before the world — which has long since devoted it to oblivion; and I have a still stronger aversion to be myself a candidate for public favour on the strength of my connection with it.'[20]

Decoding Hart's diary was an exercise in historical detection. Its most intriguing reference is to the 'Can affair'. The passage, dated 16 October 1848, reveals that Young Ireland émigrés considered an incursion into Canada — a hare-brained scheme associated usually with a section of the Fenians at the close of the American Civil War.[21] This phenomenon was rooted in American expansionism as well as Irish disaffection. Relations between the US and British North America had been stormy, with repeated unsuccessful invasions of Canada during the Revolution and the War of 1812. Moreover, the attempt to strike at Britain through Canada was supported by the United Irish exiles. In Baltimore, 'Irishmen and the descendants of Irishmen' were urged 'to complete the independence of America and shatter into pieces the chains of poor unfortunate Ireland . . . on the plains of Canada'.[22] Richard Caldwell, whose brother John met Hart, headed for the Canadian front in 1812. He raised a company of men from his new home in Orange County, New York, and marched to Canada along the Lake Champlain route. But failure in County Antrim was followed by disaster in America. Suffering from dysentery, and exposed to storms while crossing the lake, Caldwell died before reaching the Canadian border. The First New York Regiment of Riflemen (incorporating the Republican Greens) advanced with the state militia —

whose officers included Robert, son of Thomas Addis Emmet — but the US army failed to make headway in Canada.

On 4 July 1848, the 'Friends of Ireland' in Montreal held a meeting 'to make arrangements for the receipt of the brother of the martyred Mitchel and the delegate from the New York Republican Union'.[23] This delegate, Michael Thomas O'Connor, claimed to have addressed 6,000 republicans — the city was crowded with Famine emigrants — and said 'that everyone with whom he had come in contact told him that they looked forward with pleasure to the happy day when their country should become part and parcel of the United States'. Anticipating Fenian bombast, and exaggerating an economic crisis in the Canadian provinces, he declared: 'Canada must be invaded. She herself loudly demands it.' The secretary of Lower Canada (Quebec) visited the US and reported that military victory over Mexico and the presidential election had incited American aggression.[24] A group of Irish-American veterans of the Mexican war (1846–8) welcomed William Mitchel, collected $40,000 and offered their services to the Young Ireland agents. They formed the Irish Republican Union, which directed its attention towards Canada, but faded away with the collapse of rebellion in Ireland. A Boston abolitionist, writing in September 1848, observed: 'There is a class in this country not very numerous I suspect, but rather noisy and quite persevering, who will approve and aid any movement got up by anybody whatever, which looks likely to embar[r]ass the British government and cripple British power. The defeat of the Irish revolutionary schemes was a terrible extinguisher upon the hopes and plans of these men. . .' Irish-born Edward Alexander Theller, whom Hart saw (page 34), reportedly visited Boston in the late 1840s to collect money on behalf of annexationists in the Canadas. The Canadian governor general, Lord Elgin, wrote in November: 'I hear every now and then of emissaries from the New York Irish confederates, and I have reason to believe that gentry of this class are dropping in among us occasionally — but I hardly think they can have anything very serious in hand at present.'[25]

The vagueness of the scheme reflects the youth and naivety of those involved. Hart, to his credit, counselled against any 'harum-scarum expedition' got up 'to have a rap at England anywhere and collaterally to serve Ireland'. The reference in the diary at this time to 'O'G' is puzzling since Richard O'Gorman did not embark for the US until June 1849. After the rising he escaped via west Clare, Constantinople, Algiers and France. In New York he formed a successful law practice with Dillon. Kerby Miller describes O'Gorman as a classic example of the idealistic Irish political exile turned machine politician in America. He later represented the 'lace curtain' element in Irish-America. Doheny told O'Brien in 1858: 'O'Gorman is reformed and loyal and sharp as a chisel and equally keen in his race for money.' He amassed a fortune with Democratic Party 'Boss' William Tweed of Tammany Hall, survived scandals and was elected to a Superior Court judgeship. In a letter to Hart in 1888, he praised Parnell and his policy.[26]

After much discussion, indecision and inactivity, Hart's colleague Martin O'Flaherty returned to Dublin. By 1850 he was practising as a solicitor in partnership with Valentine Dillon, brother of John Blake. He dabbled later in parliamentary elections.[27] The other Young Ireland agent, William Haslett Mitchel (1830–91), also dropped out of radical politics. Hart mentions he was studying law until he got a job in Washington. Mitchel turned later to the characteristic American vocation of inventor, and designed a type-setting machine. Like his famous brother, he returned eventually to Newry, County Down.[28]

Hart's account of his meeting with Matilda Tone is of major interest. He met the widow of Theobald Wolfe Tone at her home in Georgetown two weeks before she died on 18 March 1849, aged eighty.[29] He recorded her reminiscences of Tone, Dublin and Napoleonic France. They show that her years in France (1797–1816) created a more favourable impression on her than her subsequent residence in the United States. After Tone's death Napoleon secured a pension for Matilda, which continued to be paid when she remarried and moved to the US. Hart took her advice: 'Don't expatriate yourself.' He was much impressed with the old lady, of whom Tone had written in 1796: 'On every occasion of my life I consulted her; we had no secrets, one from the other, and I unvarying found her think and act with energy and courage, combined with the greatest prudence and discretion. If ever I succeed in life, or arrive at anything like station or eminence, I shall consider it as due to her counsels and to her example.'[30]

The Young Ireland refugees included Thomas Devin Reilly, an ardent follower of John Mitchel. Shortly after his arrival in New York he started a journal called the *People*. Described as 'the most brilliant Irish newspaper . . . published in America', it was financed by William Erigena Robinson, a Tyrone-born Democratic member of Congress. When Reilly died suddenly in 1854, aged thirty, Mitchel noted in his *Jail Journal*: 'The largest heart, the most daring spirit, the loftiest genius of all Irish rebels in these latter days sleeps now in his American grave.'[31] In the first issue of the *People* Reilly reprinted an article which he had written for the first issue of Mitchel's *United Irishman*. 'The Sicilian Style' hailed the overthrow of Austrian-backed Neapolitan rule in the first revolution of 1848. It compared Sicily's decline to Ireland under the Union: 'The Sicilian peasant, like others we know of, full of natural dignity and independence, impassioned, loving, glorying in music and in song, intensely religious . . . became . . . starved, ignorant, imbecile.' Observing that the *Risorgimento* had just begun, he urged Irishmen to do their duty.[32] Reilly's article prompted reflections about 1848 which, together with spiritual pensées, form part II of Hart's diary. (Those passages, written at the back of his notebook, have been arranged chronologically in the edited text.) He recalled the unrealistic expectations raised by events on the Continent, engaged in a polemic about the state of Ireland, and concluded with a hymn in praise of his hero, George Washington, and the Irish pantheon. His sister Adelaide would write that the storm of excitement created in Ireland by the Paris revolution 'carried all before it — even the wise and calm resolves of moderate men'.[33]

[Religion — the business of knowing, loving and serving God — was for Hart 'our most important affair'. The section entitled 'religion' forms nearly one-fifth of the original manuscript. It has been severely pruned for reasons of space and because much of it reads like a pious

tract. Hart was not a careful writer and this section, in particular, ben-
efits from editing. Nevertheless, his introduction to the devout life has
an intrinsic charm and its essence has been retained. Another journal,
started in Brooklyn on 12 October 1848, shows evidence of extensive
spiritual reading.[34] It contains extracts, for instance, from the writings
of St Charles Borromeo ('there are very few who labour in earnest to
become saints'), whose feastday coincided with his birthday. He
learned from St Francis de Sales that, during 'the few years of our trial
here', nothing edifies our neighbour so much as gentleness. Hart
emerges as a dreamy, devout young man. During his travels he frequently checked Mass times with Irish (and black) servants. While
reflecting a Victorian preoccupation with duty, he believed religious
practices should be conducted with as little ostentation as possible. His
reflections on theology and cosmology are of interest as they were written a decade before Charles Darwin's *The Origin of Species* (1859).

In May 1849, Adelaide Dillon wrote to her husband that she wished
'most heartily Charles could remain in America', rather than return to
'an atmosphere of slavery' under 'that villainous government'.[35] None
the less, he was summoned home the following month. Having considered a career in farming, and been put off engineering by an
encounter with railroad inspectors who behaved like 'a set of rowdy
law clerks', he decided on the family profession. Hart entered King's
Inns to train as a solicitor, after graduating from Trinity College,
Dublin, in 1851.[36] He remained aloof from politics, unlike his brother-
in-law, who was persuaded to re-enter political life on returning to Ireland in 1856. Hart did not marry, despite advice from the former
Young Irelander, John O'Hagan, to visit Florence and bring home 'a
fair Florentine for his bride'.[37] He continued to travel on the Continent, while also sampling the spa waters in Lisdoonvarna, County
Clare, and Harrogate, Yorkshire. When Gavan Duffy returned on a visit
from Australia in 1865, he dined with a group which included Hart,
Dillon, O'Hagan and Samuel Ferguson.[38]

Dillon, by then MP for Tipperary, died suddenly the following year.
After Adelaide's death at the age of forty-four, Hart assumed an increas-

ingly paternal role towards his nephews, John and William. He joined
the newly-founded Society for the Preservation of the Irish Language
with them and served on its council for more than twenty years. The
society provided an outlet for Hart's cultural nationalism and interest
in education. In 1883 — ten years before the Gaelic League was established — he formed part of a delegation which urged the Christian
Brothers to promote Irish in their schools.[39] Following the sale of
Druid Lodge, which had a special place in the family affections, he
acquired 2 North Great George's Street in central Dublin. John Dillon
would witness the 1916 Rising from this house.

In 1885 Hart realised an ambition to visit the American west. While
game-hunting plans did not materialise, he spent more than a year on
a ranch in Castle Rock, Colorado, shaking off the symptoms of tuber-
culosis, which had probably claimed the lives of his two sisters. His
nephew William, threatened with consumption, had already gone to
live there. He continued to follow John's parliamentary career with
pride and regretted being a burden to him: 'I could however relieve
you of the trouble, distasteful probably to you, of looking after my little
properties and affairs and could live quietly and economically somewhere, not necessarily in the historical but perhaps to me somewhat
gloomy big old house [in North Great George's Street].'[40]

The defeat of Gladstone's first Home Rule Bill provoked an unchar-
acteristic outburst. William had ridden out from Denver with a telegraphic report of proceedings in London, where the measure was
defeated by 341 to 311, 93 Liberals voting with the majority. Hart wrote
to John next day: 'Hartington is a pig, Chamberlain a scoundrel, Goschen
a "gallows old rogue" and "gombeen man" (moneylender and usurer) tho'
a clever one.'[41] The Tories were 'false rascals'. He acknowledged, with
lingering naivety, that the prospects of a parliament in Dublin enhancing
the value of his house 'do not now rest on any very solid foundation'.

Four years later, on the day the Irish Parliamentary Party split
because of the Parnell divorce crisis, Hart wrote to Anne Deane: 'I am
beginning to be almost tired of politics and of debates and discussion
and grand old men and all that sort of thing. Really, Parnell seems as if

he could not be put down. I cannot bear to strain my mind much more but must try to wait patiently the course of events. I only wish John were clear out of the whole mess. . . It's a horrible mess altogether, so totally different from anything we expected a short time ago.' He added three days later: 'Certainly P. is a splendid fighter . . .'[42] John Dillon, on a fund-raising mission for evicted tenants, wrote 'in a state of uncertainty' from New York: 'How Balfour, Chamberlain and Co. must be enjoying it all. The unfortunate Irish, they display a demonical vigour and ferocity in fighting each other.'[43]

'Good Uncle Charles' shared the family grief when William Dillon's two boys died of scarlatina. William wrote stoically: 'It is not, of course, a very satisfactory or consoling thought to us to know that we have lost our two little boys mainly through the ignorance and incompetence of our local doctor.' Despite this adversity, he went on to open a law office in Chicago, edit a Catholic newspaper, and write a two-volume biography of John Mitchel.[44] Besides advancing £1,500 to his nephew, Hart donated £225 for a Catholic church in Castle Rock. The priest assigned to it described the church as 'a little gem' but failed to turn up to say Mass. The bishop's secretary explained apologetically: 'Poor Father Cummings has fallen by the way . . . drink is his curse.' William commented: 'I trust the bishop will do better for us the next time.'[45]

In the closing months of his life Hart experienced hard times. He was issued with a High Court writ in June 1898, as the surviving trustee of a marriage settlement made over thirty years before. The children of that marriage, claiming he had failed to add their mother's bequest to the estate, sued for £2,000. Hart, who was notoriously absent-minded, had neglected the trust through 'ignorance and inadvertence'. In the opinion of his counsel there was no answer to the claim made against him, even 'tho' not a penny of the money was ever paid or entrusted to me'.[46] Hart was 'much cast down and troubled and ill able to afford [the] loss'. He tried not to be depressed, 'but bad enough. It is "hard times".' He explained to his nephew that when induced to become a trustee in 1866, he was an 'imperfectly educated lawyer and just then at the end of my professional career and fit only to dabble in my own little leases, etc.' In a curiously enigmatic letter, John had written: 'I am very doubtful as to the wisdom of you going down to collect the King's Co. rents. . .'[47] John's wife, who lived in her uncle-in-law's house, found the matter 'wearisome' during the latest pregnancy. Elizabeth Mathew Dillon wrote in her diary: 'We are very much afraid he will lose this money — and it will seriously cripple *our* resources if his income and consequent contribution is so heavily curtailed.'[48]

Hart had a stroke on 12 October 1898. As it was not possible to move him, two nurses were employed and his third nephew, Father Nicholas, was summoned from Multyfarnham Friary. John had just returned from Glasgow, where he delivered 'a speech of manly courage' about healing the Parnell split. [49] Charles Hart died two days later. The attendance at his funeral in Kilmacktolway included the nationalist MPs, John Redmond and Timothy Harrington. Elizabeth Dillon was surprised that her husband mourned him so much, 'for the old man had been sadly failing lately and it was becoming very difficult to manage for him and to bear with him. But John and he had shared the same house for more than forty years and he was the last of the older generation belonging to John's mother.' Hart left all he possessed equally between Willie and John — 'this house being specified in John's share' — with a legacy to his Franciscan nephew. What each share would amount to 'depends on whether the threatened law-suit about trust money, which we are sure shortened his days, is persevered in by these unscrupulous people named Mahon'. [50]

Hart received no glowing obituaries and only one public encomium, but several people wrote to John Dillon, including Matthew Russell, SJ, founder-editor of the *Irish Monthly*; William Delany, SJ, president of University College, Dublin; and J. S. Conmee, 'the decentest rector that was ever in Clongowes', according to James Joyce.[51] Amy M. Mander, an English supporter, wrote from Letterfrack, County Galway: 'I know you will feel his loss acutely — for he was more than a Father to you. Such tender love and quiet devotion as his are the precious treasures in life. . .' An Augustinian friar described Hart as 'a Christian gentleman and a true Irishman. He always spoke of you in terms of affection and

pride.' A Limerick correspondent said he 'was one of the men of ster-
ling worth, who often keep in the back scenes of life and enjoy the lux-
ury of doing good quietly and unobtrusively'.[52]

The council of the Society for the Preservation of the Irish Language,
with Count George Noble Plunkett in the chair, passed a resolution
unanimously:[53]

> That the Council of the Society for the Preservation of the Irish Lan-
> guage, having learned with extreme regret of the death of Mr Charles
> Henry Hart, AB, who for more than twenty years has been a mem-
> ber of the Council, and from 1879 to 1886 was Hon. Treasurer of the
> Society, do now adjourn as a token of respect to his memory, and to
> mark their appreciation of his personal character and of his services
> to the Society, and do further desire to tender to his family their sin-
> cere sympathy and condolence in the loss they have sustained.

Editorial note

The aim is to present the diary as favourably and faithfully as possible.
Hart had one thing in common with the diarist Samuel Pepys: his punc-
tuation — except for hyphens — was almost non-existent. Long and
complex subordinate clauses, the product no doubt of a classical education, required clarification. Sentence and paragraph breaks have been
introduced. His text is peppered with contractions, to indicate all of
which would have required the constant use of square brackets. Therefore, frequently recurring words are spelt out silently in the edited
text, as are ampersands and numbers under 100. The manuscript is also
dotted with 'et ceteras', which have been omitted where they serve no
useful purpose. In the interests of an uncluttered narrative, many obvious errors have been corrected silently. Repetitious or trivial words and
phrases are elided, while a summary of larger deletions is provided.
The document has been reduced from approximately 31,000 words to
27,000.

The Diary of Charles Hart

[TCD, Dillon Papers, MS 6464]

Dramatis Personae

A	Adelaide ('Ady'), sister; wife of John Blake Dillon
P	Pauline ('Poll'), sister
Mr O['H]	William O'Hara, uncle and guardian
[M]O['F]	Martin O'Flaherty, Young Ireland agent
[W]M	William Mitchel, Young Ireland agent
J[B]D	John [Blake] Dillon
SO'B	William Smith O'Brien

Friday, 28 July [1848]

Took leave of all at Druid Lodge. Never can forget the deep affection and anxiety of dearest M[amma]. Was almost more affected by the emotion of warm affectionate Mr O['Hara]. Could hardly refrain from crying till got on the road where nobody could see me. Shook hands in real goodwill with poor A[delaide] at the hall door. Should not omit to mention the courage and cheerfulness of H[enry Hart, cousin?] and P[auline][1] at parting. Kept me up a good deal. Was much affected going up the road on my way in the car. Tore recipe for making [gun]powder out of my pocket book and gave it to John [presumably a servant] to take back.

Saw an ill-looking man near [Dalkey] atmospheric railway terminus, who I was sure was a detective. He came after me to the ticket office — listened when I asked for a ticket to know where I was going — and took a ticket for Kingstown. He went into the third class, I suppose to pretend that he was not watching me. I got out at Kingstown and, knowing of old the punctuality of the steamer, darted up the steps with one of the porters carrying my trunk. Just as I got in sight of the Holyhead steamer, saw her move off from the jetty and wheel out into the harbour.

I had just given my trunk to another porter. For a moment I was in despair. Some men near shouted to run on myself — and let him follow as fast as he could. I did so and the captain, who was standing on the paddle box of the steamer (by this time in the middle of the harbour), shouted 'get a boat' and stopped the vessel. I instantly made towards the boats, guided and surround[ed] by three or four boatmen. After some scrambling I finally got fixed trunk and all in a boat and was rowed off to the vessel. I was hoisted in neck and heels and my trunk after me — and away we went.

I never felt so relieved in my life. I had already, when I saw the steamer going, almost felt the gripe of Inspector O'C on my collar for I saw my friend the detective set off, as I thought, to the police office. I felt, as well I might, extremely grateful to the captain for his civility and took the earliest opportunity of thanking him. He was an exceedingly nice old gentleman, a navy officer as I judged from his manner. He told me the last news about the 'disturbances' — and lent me that morning's *Saunders's [News-letter]* to read. I thought to myself I was much wiser and knew more than either he or *Saunders's*. And tho' they said all was quiet, I felt pretty sure that all was *not* quiet. How sure we were of the people!

Came to the end of my voyage without any further adventure except being rather sick for part of the time. Tried the Quinine once and thought it did me no good, so as it was very disagreeable did not try it any more. The morning was most beautiful and the view of the Bay of Dublin and the sea and mountains surpassingly so. I looked on them with a deep and melancholy interest — what is it all but the beautiful inanimate clay without the soul. Shall I ever or under what circumstances shall I land here again. Is it possible that those few young men are at length to free this beautiful country, for which so many brave and true spirits have struggled in vain. I felt that the issue was very doubtful, but I distinctly recollect I never for one moment doubted that the people would fight. I felt quite fond of the old captain when he seemed quite proud of the beauty of the bay.

Arrived at H[oly] Head. Agreed with my two fellow travellers, the one a young Englishman, whom I took for a commercial traveller and who I afterwards discovered had whatever he was travelled a great deal, the other apparently a travelling Missionary or emis[s]ary of a bible society, to take some conveyance together to Bangor as there was no coach till a late hour. After some difficulty and higgling of course and fighting the landlord who wanted to rob [us], which I left to my English friend, we got a capital outside car.

Started for Bangor having first refreshed. I got some bread and butter and cold water, for which I paid sixpence. Got along very merrily — beautiful road. I sitting by myself enjoying the fresh air and comparing the comfortable, prosperous appearance of everything with the state of Ireland. We met people in hundreds in every direction in their best clothes — sitting and walking and driving — returning from a great camp meeting held annually for religious purposes. Some distinguished preachers attend. The substantial, comfortable appearance of these people formed a strange contrast to that of our people. Our London friend, who was paymaster, remarked that he did not wonder at the Welshmen having rebelled against the turnpikes. If he were an inhabitant he would be disposed to rebel too 'they are so numerous and expensive'.

Full view of Snowdon all the way and fine bold range of mountains. Saw train making trial trip to Holyhead railway. Got at half way another car and horse, an inside car. Now got into conversation with my English friend. Found that he was nearly as great a traveller as myself and had actually been in Rome the same winter that we were. So got on admirably talking together of 'furrin part[s]', etc. Passed the Menai bridge — certainly a most wondrous work. 'The more I gazed the more my wonder grew.' Country about very pretty. Saw at a short distance up the straits the ponderous pillars intended to support Stephenson's poor tutor. . . [2]

Came at last to Bangor, or rather to about half a mile from it to the railway terminus. Could see the little town under me. Felt a variety of sad and still some pleasing emotions thinking of pleasant times long ago. Remembered so distinctly being there when quite young going to see Snowdon. From that passed many tunnels, came to Conway. R[ail] W[ay] passes through part of the old castle but does not materially injure it. Positively one of the most magnificent and impressive old buildings in the world. One cannot call it a ruin it is so perfect. Here too old recollections came over me. . . I remembered even the very feelings with which I looked from the lofty battlements down to the beautiful suspension bridge . . .

I was then a child and those with me were comparatively young. Here we are all now how changed and at this moment embarked in an important and dangerous cause — as I then thought — not knowing under what circumstances or if we shall ever be all together again. Obliged to listen and to give a silent assent to the ignorant and prejudiced remarks of fellows in the train.

It began to be very cold. My fellow traveller and I made ourselves 'so sociable' — I giving him a share of my cloak. Came to Chester, bid goodbye to my companions and proceeded to mine inn — Tea Bell. Up in the morning and off to L[iver]pool by 9 o'c. train. When landed from ferry in Liverpool marched about five miles to the Railway Hotel to mislead the enemy, a porter carrying my trunk before me. Left my trunk there and said I would return to take luncheon.

Sallied forth to buy a watch key, having left mine behind me and having been obliged to borrow one from the waiter at Chester. Bought a night shirt which had also forgotten. Put on a grand business-like face and then went down to find out the office of the American steamers. Felt rather uneasy, suspecting everyone to be a detective and, really, the people did seem to look very hard at everybody and to be in general very much on the *qui vive*. I found the place at last and engaged my place, representing myself as a young man having a certain sum of money for a trip and anxious to make the most of it.

Returned to the hotel with a dignified nonchalance, sat down to write a letter home. Was in a little room from which could see the hall. Saw suspicious-looking fellows, as I thought, coming in occasionally. Have no doubt they were on the watch for any dangerous persons coming into the town. Was rather annoyed by the waiter asking me when I was going, what train, etc. At last I said I was going by the steamer — he still persevered and said 'the Dublin steamer?' I said yes to get rid of him. Got luncheon and passed away the time poorly enough reading old newspapers till 4 o'c. Sent for a cab and when got in told him to drive to the slip where the tender for the *Acadia* was to start from. Saw various bodies of volunteers and pensioners parading the streets looking very warlike; I of course looked at them very benevolently. [3]

Got to the slip and into the tender under the Stars and Stripes and was finally shipped after considerable delay. Started at 7 o'c. Here I was safe and sound, having got so far by various skilful stratagems. Was rather disappointed at the accommodation in second [class] cabin and numbers in it. Evening beautiful, staid up till late. When got up next morning became very sick. Was sick then more or less for a whole week; scarcely got up except for a very short time each day for a change. (Little thought when starting that that very day [29 July] fight at Ballingarry.) Weather very bad for a week.

Sunday, 6 August

Beautiful calm day. Got up and was quite well and in best spirits, little thinking or imagined about poor SO'B's state that day.[4] Protestant service on board for crew and such of passengers as liked. One of passengers, an American who did not attend, said to me that it was a tyranny to make the crew attend whether they liked or not. (Name of this gentleman was Mr Hepworth of Cincinnati — real Yankee. Told me that his grandfather had served thro' the Revolutionary war and had walked barefoot on the snow with Arnold's celebrated expedition — seemed proud of it.[5]

Whole of succeeding week tolerably fine. Some of the days beautiful; saw whales blowing at distance from ship; could just see water squirting up but could not see body of whale. On another occasion whale passed quite close to ship; showed a good deal of its body when a little astern. Another day saw a shark quite close under the side of the ship, his fin standing straight up out of the water. Could see his form just below the surface, lying quietly with his head towards the ship as if taking a survey of her as she passed. Saw his fin over the waves now and then for some time astern. Met another day a large English merchant ship in full sail, a magnificent sight. (Should have mentioned before that while I was sick just got up in time to see Cape Clear enveloped in mists or at least looking very misty and hazy — last I saw of Ireland.)

Spent the week on the whole rather pleasantly, tho' began to get dreadfully tired of it towards the end. Walking up and down, chatting, going to meals, reading *Frazer's Mag.*, the only book I could get. Looking at some passengers shooting at a bottle hung over the yardarm with one of Colt's revolvers, which now saw for the first time. Passengers very gay, chiefly American, French and German, used to sing a good deal, particularly in the evening and in the smoking room or on deck — 'Carry me back . . .' Sometimes had the *Marseillaise* or *Mourir pour la patrie* — singing all together, a young Frenchman leading. He used to become perfectly inspired; it was the most exciting thing I ever witnessed. I could now understand all I ever heard of the effects of the glorious hymn. The tears always came into my eyes when singing with them. I believed that something glorious at least had occurred or was occurring in Ireland at that moment.

Some of these young Frenchmen are very nice fellows. Their manners are so pleasing, so unaffected and easy of approval, so polite and still so manly. Company of musicians, the Moravian Minstrels, on board and on some fine evenings sing for us. Two German brewers from St Louis on board. One had been back to see his father in Bavaria for the last time. Had come out eighteen years before, had been a soldier in the States army against the Indians, had worked in a brewery and finally set up one for himself, and was doing well and was the picture of happiness and jollity.

The other had been a wealthy brewer in Germany, had got into a scrape with the excise and fled to America. His wife, whom he left in Germany, refused notwithstanding his repeated solicitations to follow him out when he got settled there, so he got a divorce and married again and so did she . . . [*details of legal battle for custody of son, with whom he was returning 'in triumph', c. 100 words*]

There was also a little Frenchman who had fought in the national guard in Paris during the insurrection of June. Told me that at one time on turning a corner they were suddenly fired upon and thirty or forty of his corps were killed. Mentioned some instances of treachery, corporals making away with ammunition. Seemed to be a great traveller in South America, etc. Told me of three weeks' calm under the tropics, dreadful depression of spirits, wine used to be mixed with water and left in buckets full for the crew to drink.

Met on deck a gentleman, apparently an Englishman. His name I believe was Reynolds. He had lived a good deal at Florence. Knew Mr J[ohn] O'H[agan][6] very well, often dined there . . . spoke very highly indeed of [him] . . . Showed me the national Italian colours — red, green and white — set in gold in concentric circles, the whole about the size of a common watch keep, now usually worn as an ornament in Italy . . .

Met others, Americans, on ship; a good deal of curiosity about Ireland and universally great sympathy and anxiety for her success. All this seemed so novel and strange to me that felt quite happy. My Cincinnati friend thought there was nothing like the Rifle and bowie Knife, and that 100,000 Yankees armed in this way would take and hold all England.

Friday, 11 August
Got into Halifax [Nova Scotia], prettily situated, two or three war steamers. Was greatly disgusted at seeing some [British] soldiers the same as ever keeping guard on one of the slips. Walked up thro' the town to the fort which is very large and strong. Steamer remained scarcely one hour — was just back in time. Was shown the Catholic Cathedral from the steamer: round building.

Came within ten miles from Boston by Sunday morning, when we were obliged to stop and lie at anchor by a fog. Lay all Sunday, got lines to fish but caught nothing. Were visited two or three times by a ferry boat which passed near. I now saw for the first time the curious American Ferry or riverboat. Passengers became outrageous [*recte* outraged] at not being allowed to land in this ferry boat. Held a meeting as is usual on all occasions here and passed resolutions . . .

Monday, 14 August
Morning fog cleared and we sailed up to Boston. Found that we had just stopped in time the previous day; a little farther and we should have run ashore. Looked with much interest at the people, etc., as land came near and landed with very peculiar feelings . . . Rather funny could not get anyone to carry out our luggage from Custom H[ouse] so had to help one another. Three of us got together, Cincinnati, myself and another, went to the station, got carriage, drove thro' town. Was instantly reminded of [Charles] Dickens'[s] idea of its being like the scenes at a pantomime.[7] Drove to Bunkers [*recte* Bunker], or rather Bruds [Breed's], Hill. It was on Breed's that the battle was fought and it is on it that the monument is erected to Warren, etc.[8] The Americans retreated to Bunker Hill and somehow the name Bunker Hill has become historical, tho' it is the other which is held sacred. The view of the city and surrounding country from Breed's [is] beautiful and must have inspired the combatants in no small degree with patriotic ardour.

Heat was very great, came back and dined. Was rather amused at getting a drink of ale with ice in it. Ice water, ice in everything. The climate would be insufferable without all this ice. Took leave of my Cincinnati friend with a warm invitation if ever I 'came West' to remember him. I saw him into the train. Delighted him by telling him who and what I was, he being a thoroughgoing Republican.

Came away in another train for N[ew] Y[ork] shortly after. Thought the railway travelling very agreeable. Should not omit that was a little surprised to see the trains running through the streets in Boston; coaches and cars crossing right before the engine when it stops for a moment just as they would do with any other vehicle. Altogether in this country they do not treat railway train engines with any of the respectful awe which is paid to them with us. Boston presented to me a very extraordinary appearance from the numberless little funny engines and trains running in all directions, and the equally numberless wooden causeways crossing the creeks or arms of the sea by which the city is separated from its suburbs. Every[thing] has a peculiarly bright neat appearance and there are many very fine houses . . .

Came off on the railway after dinner. Found the road excellent and the cars very comfortable. Felt very indignant at the misrepresentation of English travellers (but I believe that till very lately the railways fully justified their criticism). Admired as I went along the pretty New England villages, thinking that I might probably be passing thro' the very scene of the battle of Lexington [1775] (this I believe was not the case). Was at first disappointed at the careless slovenly modes of farming in use there; nothing like neatness or nice enclosures but everything careless and irregular as if they did not care how much land they wasted. Just like a fine joint of meat with the more dainty pieces cut and the whole mauled and spoiled, as if it had been laid before a person who was a bad carver and not very hungry. All this arises from the superabundance of land in the country.

Got into boat at Alleyn's Point and sailed down the sound. Was amazed at the extraordinary rapidity of the steamer far exceeding anything I had ever seen, also at its size and magnificence. The *Knickerbocker* is not by any means the finest in this line; they go at twenty-five miles an hour. Got into NY at six in the morning and drove to the Astor, where I had been advised to go by some fellow passengers. Got a room about forty flights up at the very top of the house, all the others being full.

Friday, 15 September 1848
[Martin] O'F[laherty], [William] M[itchel] and I determined to make a trip to see the Highlands of the Hudson. Started at 5 o'c. on steamer for West Point — agreed to travel as 'Brown', 'Smith', 'Jones'. Evening cold; met numbers of sail boats loaded with timber, some with bricks; amazing how low they were sunk in the water. Passed Fort Washington at ten miles from NY to the right as you go up the Hudson. Here the Telegraph Wire is stretched across the river. Close to F. Washington is C. O'Connors [*recte* Charles O'Conor's][9] country seat, just next to the telegraph wire. Evening gloomy till the moon rose. The effect was then most beautiful, particularly when we came into the highlands. Compared the scenery to Killarney.

Danced up and down the deck to keep ourselves warm in preference to going into the close cabin. Also boxed and fought. Observed Phosphoric light in water. When we came near to W. Point scenery very like Diachenfils [*recte* Drachenfels, near Bonn]. Arrived at W. Point at 10 o'c., distance from NY about fifty miles.

Landed at wooden jetty; boat stopped one minute, put out a plank, let us out and away. Found ourselves at the bottom of a steep wooded hill. Could just see the tops of the chimneys of a house thro' the trees at an immense height above us. Scrambled up a steep winding path and finally steep wooden steps to a great height thro' trees and brushwood, and found ourselves on the flat top of the height forming a pretty extensive plain, on which is an excellent hotel. At the opposite extremity is the military school and the plain between is the exercise ground. Walked across the exercise ground, looked at the cannon, observed rear triggers. Slept I in dance-room.

Saturday, 16 September

Immediately after breakfast walked out and ascended the hills which rise from the plain above mentioned till we came to the remains of the fort, the same of which Arnold had the command and which he had treacherously agreed to betray when he was prevented by the capture of André.[10] Situation is most commanding, reminded me strongly of the ruins of the old castles on the Rhine at Drachenfels, or the ruins of the Alte Schloss in Baden-Baden. Must have been almost impregnable from the great steepness of hill on which it stands.

While lying in the grass on the top of the ramparts and adoring the glorious river . . . the noble Hudson, to the left and right with villages and rising towns on its banks, thought how beautiful and sublime it must have appeared to the first discoverers; and how little perhaps they thought of the great country, of which the Hudson forms an important feature, [and the part it] would one time play in the world. Thought with deep interest of the important event in the Revolution connected with this plain. In ascending the rude stone steps leading to the platform on which we were lying, thought that it was almost certain that André had gone up those very steps when making his plan of the fortress. Looked up the Hudson wondering where it was he had endeavoured to cross. Talked over the stern integrity and patriotism of the militia men who captured him. Argued whether the employment of a spy in military matters was not honourable. Agreed that it was, but that inducing treachery in any of the opposite party *was not* . . . [*Mitchel cuts branch of tree growing in the ruined fort 'as a relic' and divides it with Hart.*]

Thought how admirably the plain below had been selected as the site of the National Military College. Keeping the beauties and great natural advantages of their country before the eyes of the students, together with the recollections belonging to a plain associated with so critical an event in their country's history. Came down the hill and stood to see the students or cadets marching to their classrooms. Fine straight well-looking lads most of them. Their uniform a light grey military coat with very small tails, large brass knobs and white duck trousers, a glazed leather cap — altogether very becoming — their demeanour very orderly and gentlemany.[11] None of the aristocratic or would-be aristo-cratic insult or misbehaviour observable amongst English boys . . . [*polite young soldier shows them way into library.*]

The Library composed in great measure of military and scientific works, also histories, etc. Full-length portraits of [Thomas] Jefferson — an elegant as we would say most aristocratic-looking old man, a slight look of Henry Grattan, the elder — and of [James] Munroe, afterwards president, also a fine-looking man but not very intellectual looking. I was interested in him as I gather he was ambassador Munroe, poor Tone's friend in Paris [in 1796]. Portrait of [John Caldwell] Cal-houn[12], very fine mild intellectual face. Bust of Washington and of Lafayette[13], latter poor face.

Walked up to the burial ground, very prettily situated. Returned and walked over to a white marble pillar overhanging the river and to our surprise and delight found inscribed on it the name 'Koscuisko' [*recte* Kosciusko].[14] A soldier standing by showing it to some friends told us that it was Kosciusko who had chosen this spot as a site for a mil-itary college, that he had been in this country and in the service of the government as military engineer. We all agreed how admirable his taste and how true his judgement for, as M[itchel] remarked, that being brought up in the midst of fine scenery has a most beneficial effect on the mind.

Came away at half past 7 o'c. in a steamboat crowded as never was steamboat before. It was an opposition boat and we got down the fifty miles for 25 cents or one shilling, which explains the crowd. Great part of the passengers Irish in all stages of improvement, from the lately arrived to the old settler. None were however emigrants, all were more or less well off. One cabin was devoted to and entirely filled with ladies. River smooth as glass — beautiful band on board — got back to NY 5 p.m. Strange to say felt in walking through the Battery Park to the South Ferry as if I were at home again, tho' I am so short a time here. What creatures of habit we are.

Felt when sailing up the Hudson how strange, here I am in the midst of those scenes of which I have been reading all my life, but little thought I should ever see even three months ago. Once or twice occurred to me on that vast river and looking over the dark wooded country, that in the great material prosperity which is so universal in this country we are apt to forget our Creator and the better world for which this, even under all the advantages which it possesses in this country, is but a preparation. I also felt that (I do not know what it was exactly that brought the idea into my head, whether it was the grandeur and vastness of the river and scenery — tho' there doesn't seem to be any natural connexion) even in this country there are difficulties to be encountered and miseries to be endured; and that man with all the advantages and liberty he endures [*recte* enjoys], and self-reliance he manifests, is still even here weak and frail and dependent.

Sunday, 17 [September 1848]
Nothing partic[ular]. Went to Mass to St Mary's. Remarked vulgarity and almost rudeness of well-dressed Irish people. Originally poor and degraded, dress and a little prosperity can not make people refined all at once.

Monday, 18 [September]
Read and began to write my journal. Went in the evening to the Library in Broadway and began [to read George] Bancroft['s ten-volume history of the United States].

Tuesday, 19 September
Wrote short letter home, speaking of not having got any letters for two weeks. Walked in the afternoon with Mrs B and Mrs H[15] and M[itchel] to Greenwood cemetery — the finest perhaps in the world in situation, character of ground, planting. About three miles from Brooklyn saw military funeral of . . . a volunteer shot by a guerrilla in Mexico. Scene very impressing from situation, noble view of the harbour, setting sun, etc. Came back in stage[coach].

Wednesday, 20 September
Read novels of [James Fenimore] Cooper. Wrote some. Walked in afternoon with O['Flaherty], who had not been before, and M to Greenwood and all about. Had some difficulty to humbug the old man at the gate, an Irishman, to let us in but succeeded at last. Walked about a good deal. In walking back got a tremendous shower of rain, the first good wetting I had got since I came here.

Thursday, 21 September
Read and took walk in morning. Went to NY [from Brooklyn in the] afternoon, bought map and guide book of States. Read Bancroft till dark in Library.

Friday, 22 September
Read and wrote in the morning. Spent afternoon in Library at Bancroft. Inquired about confession at church near Astor Hotel. After tea heard cannon fired. Thought it was the steamer from Bremen and [Le] Havre. M and I went across to NY. Saw rockets thrown up, was nothing but a [Zachary] Taylor [presidential campaign] meeting in N[ew] Jersey.

[*The next entry is erased and part of page removed; pages 18 and 19 are likewise missing, while page 20 has also been crossed out.*]

Sunday, 24 September
Made a trip on Haarlem Railway . . . [with O'Flaherty, Mitchel and W, a newly-arrived émigré]. Rambled a few miles thro' the country, knocking down apples growing at the roadside with stones and chatting. Dined at a small country inn. Returned to town. Took a swim at the Battery. Took tea in Broadway and walked all together in the park till a late hour, talking over Ireland, SO'B, etc., with the deepest interest.

Tuesday, 26 September
Got money — ready to start for Niagara next day. Paid that evening board, etc., and O['Flaherty] and I packed a few things for each in our carpet bag.

Wednesday, 27 September
Started early in the morning, reached the Albany steamboat at 7 o'c. Breakfasted on board. Reached Albany that evening — slept there. Felt a remarkable change in climate, much colder than NY. Getting up early in the morning was reminded strongly of being in Germany, the cold frosty air, the dress and appearance of the people, the chopping of wood everywhere.

Started after breakfast for Buffalo; dined at Syracuse; went on till night. Were delayed by a bridge which was said to be broken and had to stop at 2 o'c. at night at Rochester. Slept sitting by the stove till morning. After breakfast started for Buffalo. Walked about for an hour and started for Niagara. Got there night of Friday . . . On the way felt as if one were in the middle of a clearing, all the fields being full of stumps sticking up everywhere and the forest surrounding on every side at a short distance. The land on the banks of the Mohawk River, along which the railway ran for the first day after leaving Albany, is perfectly cleared and like the meadows in our own country. It is also very rich. [The railway] ran for a good way near the Erie canal. Vast trade and number of boats.

Saturday, 30 September
Got up in the morning and looked out the window. First thing I saw was the cloud of mist rising from the fall and a beautiful rainbow formed in it by the rising sun. After breakfast sallied out to see the falls. Saw the American fall, then crossed [in] the ferry to the Canadian side to see the Horseshoe, burning springs, Table rock. Met Irish driver. On our return bought at Niagara on American side some Indian curiosities. On the whole thought falls, tho' very wonderful, rather tame. O['Flaherty] greatly disappointed. In the evening walked down the Niagara River to the Suspension bridge. Found that a fight had taken place that morning and that one end was now in the possession of the company, the other on the American side in that of the contractor. Walked on the bridge as far as the middle, where the planking had been torn up and a barricade erected by the contending parties.

Sunday, 1 October

Was told by Negro Boots that could hear Mass in Niagara in Mrs Looby's. But found when it came to the point, having held a council of all the Irish servants in the place, that there was no priest to come that day to Niagara. So had to say prayers at home.

Happened to turn into the newspaper room in the hotel and read in a Buffalo paper a telegraphic report of the most serious disturbances in Ireland, engagement at Portlaw.[16] Thought at first it was a ridiculous *rechauffe* of the old business, but soon perceived that it was not. Ran up in the greatest agitation to O. Both got into considerable [state] of excitement. Had previously determined to leave at half past 2 o'c.; waited impatiently for an hour; walked out down the river for a short time. Had laid out to sail up in the *Maid of the Mist* today, but forgot all about it till had discussed the news and it was then too late. Believe also that she was laid up for the season on Saturday evening.

Started . . . east for Lewistown. On the way got a grand view of a vast extent of forest, and of a fine and well-cultivated plain near the banks of the Niagara River. At L. got into steamer for Oswego. Sailed down Niagara into Lake Ontario. Observed at a short distance from mouth of river remarkable difference between two little towns, one on the British side dilapidated and miserable looking, everything about seeming neglected and decaying; the other on the American side exactly opposite, quite flourishing and bright warehouses and little wharves. Three or four nice little trading schooners and two steamers lying up by the town and every appearance of comfort. Not a single keel on the British side except the stranded wreck of an old steamer that seemed to be falling to pieces from *mere inanition!* And close to the water's edge, where there is a ferry, two or three soldiers pacing up and down and a sentry box close at hand.

At the mouth are two forts, one on the American the other on the British side. On the latter I saw, the first time for some weeks, the pirate flag of the bloody old British Empire. We now were out on Lake Ontario. Our course lay along the American shore at a few miles' distance. The shore, as long as one had light to see, seemed to be studded with farmhouses and to be cleared a short way in, but still the same dark line of wood was always in the background, here and there extended down to the water's edge. Concluded that the soil must be very good along the shore of the lake. To the north one could of course see nothing but a vast expanse of water like a sea or ocean. When the night came on it blew very hard and finally we had as great a storm as ever I experienced.

Reached Oswego six or seven hours later than we should have done at 11 o'c., and set off on what is called the plank road to Rome [NY]. Something like mail coach travelling. The road is planked with thick planks all the way, that is the planking is about eight feet wide and such a pleasant road. Dreadfully wet day. Found Rome filled with people, there being a court held there. All the hotels quite full, so after supper went on in railway and got into Albany at six in the morning.

Tuesday, 3 October
Here got a paper containing fuller account of Irish affairs. Still were anxious to get back expecting letters. Went to Mansion House to breakfast and got O's umbrella, which we had forgotten when going up. Came off in boat. Wet misty day. Was asked once or twice during the day to whom I would give my vote at the next election for president. The same often happened in the railways.

It is very usual for men to go about in steamboats, railway cars, etc., collecting the votes; and then perhaps they will put the result in the papers of the vote of the passengers of such a boat on such a day having been for Taylor or [Lewis] Cass[17] as the case may be. It is said that this has some slight effect on votes. It is certainly done with that intention. The Whigs generally carry the day in steamboats, railroad cars, etc., the chief strength of the Democrats lying in the working classes who do not go about so much.

Should have mentioned that when at Niagara drove into Canada to see the ground on which the battle of Lundeys [Lundy's] Lane was fought. The position of the troops on both sides, the spot where Gen. Scott[18] stood, were all pointed out to us by our driver, an Irishman, who said he had his information from Gen. Worth, who was present at the battle and whom he said had been over the ground in his carriage one month before us. Should also have mentioned that fire seemed to have been used universally in clearing of the woods — the stumps everywhere were charred. Here and there stands up a tall tree blasted and killed by the fire, and along the skirts of the forest surrounding a clearing many trees bear the marks of fire.

Came to US Hotel, Fulton St. [New York], and slept there. Before went to bed got Europe *Times* and read full account.

Wednesday, 4 October

Went to Mr B[ill]'s to look for letters, got none, went on way. Mr Reynolds invited me to go to see him. Do not know whether will or not. On my return, when walking into the hotel, could scarcely believe when I saw [James] Cantwell walking towards me[19]. Did not know what to say felt so glad to see the poor fellow. Took him straight up to our room where O['Flaherty] was; made him sit down and tell us all he knew.

Told us about J[ohn Blake] D[illon]. He was not at Ballingarry; for after Killenaule[20], where he took a prominent part, he went off with the intention of making for his own country and C went part of the way with him. Meagher could have been got off, as several offers were made to him even by four magistrates of Waterford. But quibbles as to honour were always raised by [Maurice] Leyne[21], who clung to M[eagher] for protection and seemed to have been a broken down besotted creature. P. J. Barry[22] came to Meagher, L and [Patrick] O'D[onohue] two or three times in the hope of betraying them, till he was threatened. If it had not been for Leyne, Meagher could and would have been saved.

Mr Mackey, the priest, behaved very well; G[ore] J[ones] also behaved very honestly[23]. The police in some instances were faithful, e.g., when SO'B went to Thurles, police who knew him *well* took opportunities of passing him close and whispering: 'For God's sake, Sir, why do you expose yourself so.'

C[antwell] was hiding for many days in various places, and finally got

off from Waterford in steamer and then in emigrant vessel from Liverpool. Took C to see M[itchel] and returned to our old quarters.

Thursday, 5 October
Went to see drilling at Munroe Hall [accompanied by Mitchel, O'Flaherty and Cantwell].

Friday, 6 October
Went to try if any letters came by *Hermon*. Got one for O from J[ohn]
E[dward] P[igot][24] . . . Nothing of importance in it. There was an
enclosure from A[delaide], just a few words.

    Saw Theller here for the first time. Keen looking man, very like a
little friar. . .

Sunday, 8 October
C and I went to Mass together in South Brooklyn. I afterwards dined
with Dr H. Heard of Dr [William] Walsh of Halifax[25] being in town and
went with Dr H after dinner to see him at Dr Hughes['s][26]. Failed in
seeing either.

Monday, 9 October
Went with W to see *Garrick*, the vessel in which he came out. Went to
look for Dr Walsh at an hotel where I heard he was. Did not find him.
Afternoon went to see Mrs B, who was upstairs ill. Met for the first
time Finlay, nice little fellow. Went afterwards to see Mr B to speak
about Cantwell.

Tuesday, 10 October
Took C to Exchange and introduced him to Mr B, who very kindly
promised to assist him in getting a situation as far as he could. I gave him
a letter which O had written to Mr Ingoldsby. Felt much pleasure in
doing any little thing in our power for C, whom we believe to be a very
honest respectable young man.

Thursday, 12 October
Met C in town. He said he had seen Mr Ingoldsby that morning and that nothing could exceed his kindness. Took him to the mercantile reading room and made him free of it for one month. Kept O['Fla-herty]'s letter to show to his friends. O, M and I walked about the Battery till pretty late, came home by the South Ferry.

Friday, 13 October
Went to see Dr Walsh, having first ascertained where he was staying by enquiring at the bishop's house. Knew me at once, looked remarkably well. Asked for all my friends . . .

Took the liveliest interest in my account of late transactions in Ireland. Said he had read everything that could bear upon the subject, but had not had anything like a true idea of affairs till now. Said of Meagher: 'Poor Tom, I often nursed him on my knee when he was a child.' Was much surprised when he heard that JD was my brother-in-law. Said he had heard so much and favourably of him. Used the expression: we have heard so high a character of him. Chatted over everything for at least three hours. Brought in Mrs Boyle and two nieces to introduce them, Misses Foley; very kind and very Irish. Mrs B looks very well.

Dr Hughes came in and I was introduced to him. (Dr W said he would call on me and took my direction in Brooklyn.) Dr H — clever, keen, impressive-looking man, fine head — I think a very Irish face. I could not help thinking of Gerald Griffin's description in the *Collegians*: 'A nose that in Persia would have won him a throne' . . .

[*Goes to see William Charles Macready in performance of* King Lear *that evening.*]

Should have mentioned that on my return from seeing the bishop found [John] Drumm[27] at our lodgings, having just arrived in an emigrant vessel. It would seem from some expression he made that he is disposed, in conjunction with some others, to turn his 'martyrdom' to some account in this country. In other words, to abuse the sympathy of the American people . . . [*Mitchel and O'Flaherty meet Colonel D, 'the most distinguished man in the US army'*]

Monday, 16 October

Sat at home all day, except [for] short walk, writing up my journal and reading a little. We began to abuse the old Brittanica [*recte Britannica*] which has not come in yet.

We found this morning a paragraph in the [*New York*] *Tribune* proposing a meeting to 'sympathise' with the Irish 'exiles' now in this country and giving with others the names of M and O. Both wrote letters to appear in next day's *Tribune* repudiating anything of the kind. Consider this to have emanated from Darcy McGhee [Thomas D'Arcy McGee] or his friend Mr Drumm.

Walked after tea with O['Flaherty]. Talked a good deal about Can[adian] affair. He engaged that unless proof given that feasible and likely to be successful would not engage in it, and that M[itchel] had now been sent to find out if feasible; for I represented as strongly as possible the absurdity of a man engaging in a harum-scarum expedition just because he had pledged his hand and honour to [Richard] O'G[orman], and that he would share in any danger or fate that might befall them.

On former occasions he had declared to me that could not bear the idea of living at home, even if permitted, could not endure the sneers of others, etc. Now acknowledged that from reflection, various things which have come to light, etc., his mind had changed on that point, just as I often thought it would. But said that thought it would be selfish and craven to go back quietly now, having pledged himself to M and O'G (JD, he said, he did not think it necessary to pledge himself to) to court the same fate that they might endure. He said he felt quite confident of getting leave to return as he was sure that his name had been kept out of the *Hue and Cry* by *influence* and that his professional prospects, which he used to say were ruined, would not suffer so much after all; that six months' illness at any time might have just done as much harm and that character, so far from being injured, might be rather served.

Most of these were my views which I had formerly urged and which I considered it my duty to urge in order to prevent him throwing away his life uselessly, or under any false sense of desperation at ruined fortunes which in reality does not exist. In addition to my own feelings and the recollection of all that was said to me by Mr O'H[ara], V[alentine] D[illon], etc., feel that most probably O's own relations look to me to exert influence to prevent him doing anything rash; as suspect that Mr O'H told his brother that I would do so, and most likely prevented his coming out here to try to do so himself. This I do not know but only suspect from some expression in a letter received by O from his elder brother.

We have had many conversations on *these subjects* as I feel I would be seriously to blame and would feel deeply grieved if, thro' any want of energy on my part, anything silly were engaged in. I also said that part of his feelings in the Can[adian] matter was the strong desire to have a rap at England anywhere and collaterally to serve Ireland.

Tuesday, 17 October
Steamer *Britannica* came in at 1 o'c. Went in for letters in afternoon, waited in Mr B's office till 5 o'c., as could not open the two ponderous letters directed to Mrs B in Adys [Adelaide's] handwriting. When Mr B came and opened them got the happy news of JD's escape. Felt quite happy, came home as fast as possible [to] tell O, who was overjoyed. All felt our spirits quite raised. Felt so happy too about poor O'G and O'D and D.[28] Independently of our personal feelings, it is such a triumph over the government. The more energetic men of the [Young Ireland] party have escaped, which must be the case where the population is disaffected and willing at least to thwart the government. Could not go to bed or think of sleeping till very late this night thro' excitement.

Wednesday, 18 October
Went with O['Flaherty] to see Mrs Bill. Got from her a long letter from A[delaide] to O, which Mrs B had thought was for her. She looked so well and was so overjoyed to find that JD had got off.

Had a long chat with Mrs B — she was in such excellent spirits. Rather a curious circumstance, she mentioned that many Protestant girls are educated not only at the day school of the convent of the

S[acred] H[eart] in NY, [but] also as boarders at the convent of the same order at Manhattanville.

O called on D'Arcy McGee, who has just come to NY. Did not see him but left a card. Heard today from Cantwell that Byrne, the hatter from Dublin, has been here some time, that he has been working in Philadelphia and is now in NY. Must see him and question him. Heard also from C that McGee says he got arms, etc., in Glasgow and shipped them to Sligo. Went there himself and the leaders of 2,000 Ribbonmen had agreed to rise when news reached them that SO'B and the other leaders had disagreed about quartering the people on the Landlords and they refused to strike till further news. He escaped to Derry and sailed from that [port].

Nothing of any moment occurred during the remainder of this month. We went one day to Staten Island and walked about. Met Dr Walsh from Halifax at evening parties two or three times. However, towards the end of this month got a letter from home announcing *for certain* the escape from Ireland of [J]BD . . . Wrote a letter home stating what time it took to reach America in a sailing vessel at that time of the year, as from what I could gather from their letters I felt quite sure they had underrated the length of the voyage.

Tuesday, 31 October

Went with MO'F to see Mrs B to show her a letter which I received the day before speaking most confidently of John being with us. Before now I had begun to feel a little uneasy when I saw the preceding week go over and no arrival. There had been various reports of ships having been wrecked and dismasted, turned upside down, etc., in the Gulf Stream. When this day (the last for the European post of this week) came, was in despair and resolved not to write in order not to give the government information, not knowing but he might still possibly be within their reach.

Also hoped that they would at home think my letter had gone astray or been stopped (as I then supposed many of my former ones *had* done) and that in this way they would be less uneasy than if they had a letter from me stating that he had *not* come. In this I was wrong, as I have since found that all my letters reached [Dublin] safely and regularly, so that the non-arrival of one this week would have caused a good deal of uneasiness. Had a good deal of conversation with Mrs B — were all very anxious, she very much so indeed, charged us when going away to give her the earliest information.

Went home and in a few minutes in walked John, wonderfully well considering all he had gone thro'. Looked very weather-beaten and thin. Heard all from him and need not say how happy and easy in our minds it made us all to have him safe. Next day but one went in the evening to see Mrs B — joyful meeting; poor Mr Finlay was in the greatest raptures. Paid other visits to Mrs B and C[harles] O'C[onor], R[ichard] E[mmet], etc[29].

Saturday, 4 November
Set out for Morristown in N[ew] Jersey; remained there till 7 November. In the interval met several times the priest of Madison four miles distant. Very intelligent, well-informed pleasing young man. Met Mr McQuade, son of Irish parents, excellent specimen of this class. Was deploring the want of Catholic schools for the children of Irish. They generally become good members of society but either Protestants or, more commonly, nothing at all in regard to religion, and almost invariably prejudiced and bitter against Ireland.

Those however who thro' any fortunate circumstance, such as parents having sufficient education and intelligence to teach them their religion and make them practise it, preserve the Catholic [faith. They] are almost invariably patriotic and [to] the foremost in any attempt to promote the interests of Ireland. It is obvious from this that any system of good Catholic education would be of great importance and would exercise an immense influence in this country, where the number of Catholics (chiefly Irish) is so immense and that of their children of course much more so. If these children were all properly educated and preserved in the Catholic faith it would quickly become the faith of a very large portion of the inhabitants of this country, whereas now it is chiefly confined to the Catholic emigrants and numbers but few native-born Americans.

[Fr McQuade] told us that church at Madison had been built by French who settled there after first revolution. A good many of them about there still, and also many French who fled from the late insurrection in Martinique and other West Indian islands.

Spent Sunday and Monday at Morristown and on Tuesday (the day of Gen. Taylor's election) returned to NY, having first been present for a short time at the balloting place in Morristown. Put up at the Franklin Hotel, Broadway. JD's leg not being well enough to enable him to walk about and enjoy the country and the weather being rather cold and disagreeable were the reasons which induced us to return. Walked out a little that evening to American Museum . . . Think that it was this morning in hurry and crowd at Pass office that I lost $25, the only money I have as yet lost.

M[itchel] and MO'F went to look for lodgings, found out by advertisement 341 Houston and came here same day. M remained about two weeks and then set out for Chiliaygan [Sheboygan?] in Wisconsin by advice of H[orace] G[reeley]. Cantwell decided to go with him. They stopped in Milwaukee where they now are.

[*After nearly a four-month break Hart resumes his diary in Washington, DC.*]

24 February [1849]
JBD, MO'F and myself spent time from that out reading, I chiefly algebra and engineering. JD much confined by his leg which he put under Dr McNeven's[30] care shortly after coming to Houston St. by Mr Emmet's advice. It began at once to improve under his care. It was thrown back by JD going out walking more than he should, but still on the whole improved till two or three weeks since when its improvement became less steady. After considerable time offered Dr McNeven payment and asked for account; he refused so sent him $30, of which he sent back $10 . . . When I left him on Thursday, 22 February, [Dillon] was almost quite well.

During this time C[harles]O'C[onor] had — after first showing attention on different occasions to JD . . . showing him thro' the courts himself and on more than one occasion sitting chatting in court, presenting him with cards for the Duncan dinner, asking him to dine and making a party for him, etc. — finally consulted the judges as to whether they would admit JD [to the New York State Bar] on their own authority without consulting the legislature. After a delay of some two or three weeks they decided that they could not, at the same time expressing much regret. This decision was chiefly due to a published decision made by them a short time before in which they collaterally laid down the requisites for admission, one of which was citizenship.

After a delay of another week, while CO'C was at Washington a bill drafted by him was sent to H. Greel[e]y and by him given to Gov. [William Henry] Seward, who pledged himself that it should pass the NY legislature, admitting JD to practise. This is still undone. If it should pass, which appears pretty certain, it will still be necessary to apply to the Supreme Court at Albany. When I left NY we had agreed that JD should go to Albany. I wanted to go with him as he is rather careless about his health when alone and he is not very strong and the weather cold, but he would not let me as I had been there before. MO'F decided on remaining at NY.

During this time studies, drawing, etc., much interrupted by visitors coming to congratulate JD and persons arriving from Ireland. In addition to McGee, Drumm, Cantwell, etc., who had arrived shortly before, soon after came McClinihan [*recte* John McClenahan][31], Dr [Thomas] Antisell[32], O'Hanlon, from Liverpool. [Another arrival was] Cavanagh [John Kavanagh], who was wounded at Ballingarry and who came frequently and by his strange manner left the impression that he was a rogue or was not quite in his right mind, which latter was rather confirmed when we heard from SO'B and [Terence Bellew] MacManus that he had behaved boldly and well at Ballingarry and that they believed him true. Strange tho' that when JD wrote him a note testifying as to his conduct, which he had most earnestly asked for verbally and by letter, he never acknowledged the note nor have we seen or heard of him since.

McClenahan brought out likeness of SO'B and Meagher and got them struck off here. I bought SO'B's which is very good and we have had it hung up in our room.

A poor boy named Madden, who had been at Ballingarry with SO'B, arrived here with his brother. The brother obtained some employment but [he] could get none. He is a fine boy, gives a very consistent probable account of this affair, at which JD was not present, and proves SO'B to have acted with determination and skill according to his resources. He had men employed piling hay against the rear of the house in which the police were, and those who had guns covering them by firing in at the windows which overlooked the rear, when Mr [Philip] Fitzgerald and two or three other priests came up and by the most violent moral and physical exertions drove away the people who were firing and the more easily those who were carrying the hay. SO'B even said — contrary to the false reports which were spread about him, when the Widow McCormack asked him not to burn the house on account of her children — in an excited manner: 'Oh, my good woman, never mind we'll pay for them', or something of that kind; which proves that he did not sacrifice the chance of striking a blow for such a contemptible reason as was falsely said.

We have had frequent visits from poor Madden, who has not been able to get employment nor have we succeeded in doing so for him. He was a nailer at home and well off. We have been obliged to force relief on him from time to time to keep him from starving.

One Sunday JD and MO'F went to see Mr Emmet. I remained at home and walked out with P. J. Smith [Smyth][33]. While they were there who should walk in but T[homas] D[evin] Reilly, just landed, greatly reduced by his adventures and voyage. . . The Es kept them to dinner and they had a jolly evening. They brought TDR to our lodgings, and my surprise and indeed joy to see him poor fellow were great. He staid a day or two or three till he got clothes and got well, when he removed to Brooklyn to Mrs Murrifields, our former landlady. Told us many amusing adventures. Were much amused and surprised at the Republican sort of tailor who made his clothes, who spoke so learnedly and seemed so well informed in the politics of the country. Were annoyed with his forwardness and meanness afterwards and found out that he was an office seeker.

After some time [William Erigena] Robinson, Reilly and McClenahan proposed starting a paper to be called the *People*. After some weeks it came out. After a short trial McC was found by the other two to be of no particular service to the general interest, as the branch in which he wished to occupy himself was already amply supplied by Reilly (i.e., political and literary articles), and there was a want of someone to conduct the business department which he would not do. So they compromised and separated. I thought at first that it would be useful and creditable to Ireland and Liberty generally, but I am not so sanguine now.

One Sunday morning about a month ago, just as JD, MO'F and I were going out to Mass, in walks Michael Doheny, blooming after a sojourn in France and a long sea voyage. After Mass we dined together. He was at first red hot about the priests but from the tone we took, and when he heard of the sort of fix in which McGee then was owing to his contest with the bishop, changed his tune[34]. A few nights after he had an opportunity to display his eloquence at a dinner of a military company. He talked about 20,000 pikes, etc., all which of course was true. Since then at the Bergin and Ryan dinner he made an eloquent but in many parts untrue speech, and as we are told has been constantly or at least frequently drinking.

Last Sunday night Bishop Hughes invited us to supper and also Doheny, not however by our introduction. He came quite tipsy and behaved in a very disgusting manner, brawling and disputing with Mr Brownson[35], and treating the Bishop with a rude and vulgar familiarity. We naturally felt ashamed, tho' it was impossible not to laugh. This coupled with his unhandsome and false insinuations and statements about SO'B have made us resolve not even to have pity on him for the future. The Americans who have met him seem to see thro' him pretty clearly, e.g., Mrs B and Mr B.

During this time Mr R. Dillne called and introduced himself and in
a day or two politely invited JD to sup at his house with some friends,
where he met among others Mr M. Smith, his brother-in-law. Spent a
very pleasant evening. Sometime after JD and MO'F received tickets (a
present from CO'C) to the Duncan dinner. Not long after CO'C
invited us all three to dine with him. JD and I went, MO'F did not.
Pleasant evening. Met Mr Caldwell[36], a great deal about [17]98 and
County Antrim. Dined one day long before this with Mr Emmet,
MO'F, W. Mitchel and I. Pleasant evening. Saw beautiful portrait of
Robert Emmet. Dined Sunday about three weeks since with Mr and
Mrs M. Smith — nice people. One Sunday JD and I dined with Rev Mr
McCarron at St Joseph's.

Two or three Sundays ago went by invitation to a profession of a
nun at the convent of the Sisters of Mercy opposite — very imposing.
Some time before Christmas JD and I called on Dr Walsh of Halifax
and, not finding him at home, he called on us in the evening and had a
long chat. Only a few weeks ago JD called on Dr Hughes, not finding
him at home. And he called on us some evening after with Mr McCarron. Very agreeable pleasing man. We three called again on him [a]
short time since. He then asked us to come on last Sunday evening as
before mentioned.

During this time weather up to few days before Christmas very fine,
Indian summer almost all the time. From that out frost and snow, sometimes very severe cold, occasional fine days. Sky almost always bright
and air dry and bracing. Fine sleighing on New Year's Day and for long
time before and after and often since. On that day great gaiety and vis-
iting. During this time we visited our friends, Mrs B, etc., occasionally
but indeed very seldom. Evening seems to be the favourite time for vis-
iting owing to the business habits of the people. Took walks up towards
the country occasionally . . . Took long walk in N[ew] J[ersey] to near
Newark with MO'F.

A week or ten days ago determined to go see Washington and Congress before it should rise, as it does not sit again till December. Wanted
MO'F to come but would not. Decided to set off on Thursday after Ash

Wednesday. Got letter of introduction to H[orace] G[reeley] from MO'F, came down to Jersey ferry with me. There met Sheridan, a young man whom JD and MO'F knew in Ireland. Decent fellow. He and I travelled together to Philadelphia in second class [rail carriage] — the first I had seen in this country. Snowy cold day. Parted at Philadelphia, he going where he had been directed by his friend, I to the Baltimore depot to leave my trunk. He was on his way to Madison, Indiana. After eating some dinner, having an hour to spare, I walked up and down Chestnut St., the principal street. Went into the town hall but could not for love nor money get into the room where the Declaration [of Independence] was signed, it being locked and the janitor away. Mounted the steeple, however, and saw the old bell that rang out Independence with the remarkable inscription: 'Proclaim Liberty to all this people.'

Came away in train at 4 p.m. Streets of Phil[adelphia] straight and regular and kept very clean. Whether it was the bad day or what I do not know, but do not like it as well as NY. Thought the people did not look so kind and had not so mild and inoffensive an expression of countenance.

When came to the Sasquihanna [*recte* Susquehanna River] found it covered with thick ice. Walked across in a track smoothed down purposely at each side. Ice very rough as it had broken up, drifted and heaved and tipped about and frozen hard again. Passed thro' Baltimore at twelve at night, arrived in Washington at three in the morning, went to bed at Coleman's [Hotel].

Next morning found out HG — gave my letters — civil. Went to Capitol into gallery of Ho[use] of Rep[resentatives]. First impression made was that there was a great waste of time, much more being spent in going thro' forms, dividing, calling for the 'ayes and nays', than in the transaction of business. Heard afterwards however that it was a contest between parties — the one trying to bring on certain bills, the other endeavouring to prevent them by availing themselves of every possible form and means of delay.

Went from that to the gallery of the Senate. Was struck at once by order and decorum observed there. Different from the Ho. of Reps., which was very noisy and as it seemed to me confused. This perhaps arose in some degree from the much larger number of members than in the Senate. The character of the members too was evidently very different. In the House members for the most part were plain in appearance, careless in dress and by no means except in some instances imposing or intellectual looking, tho' very many of them were sensible practical looking men enough. Some that I heard speak did not speak or pronounce well — some did well enough. There was a great appearance of carelessness and rather confusion, but certainly there was nothing particular to arrest attention. The hall of meeting is semi-circular, large and apparently well adapted for the purpose. A number of boys or lads were stationed near the steps of the elevated chair of the speaker and other officials and acted as messengers for them or any of the members. They seemed to answer the purpose very well, gliding about rapidly and noiselessly.

The appearance of the Senators was in general intellectual, many of them remarkably so. I was at once struck by Dan Webster's[37] appearance and did not need to ask who he was but knew him from his numerous likenesses. Thought he had a more practical matter of fact sort of face than the pictures give him. (I have since seen him look just like his pictures.) Saw Calhoun with his thin spectral appearance, long rather bushy hair and bright flashing eyes. Heard Webster deliver a short speech on the question of giving government to California, in which he advocated giving the President authority to govern it for the present till matters became more settled. Thought his remarks sensible, his manner modest and conciliatory. He used scarcely any gesture but for almost the whole time kept his hands hanging down before him clasped together.

Came away and wrote a letter to JD in NY — and dined very badly, as it was Friday and there was scarcely any fish or anything I could eat, tho' for everyone else a fine dinner. Walked up as far as the President's house, did not go in. From that to the Patent office but could not get in. Came back, sat near the stove reading . . . till 6.30, when there was tea. After this came to see HG again; advised me to wait till Pres.

[James] Polk's Levee on Tuesday or Wednesday. Said I ought to spend a week. Said something to him about engineering; he did not seem to know much about it; spoke of the new coal region in Virginia as worth seeing.

After this I went to hotel, paid my bill and brought my things and took a room [in] same house as HG — for which, tho' small, agreed to pay $4 for the week. Was however a great saving on the hotel at $2 a day, where could not get what I wished it being Lent, and I can live as I wish at a restaurant for 50 or 60 cents a day. Walked about for some time among the crowds waiting to see Old Jack [President-elect Taylor] come in. Rockets were thrown up [by] cannon. Shortly after Old Jack arrived and drove rapidly by, surrounded by a motley crowd of horsemen and footmen shouting, etc. Could not of course see him as it was quite dark. Went to bed early being tired, having had so little sleep night before and standing good part of the day in the Senate.

Saturday, 24 February
After breakfast went up to Patent office. Spent upward of two hours there. Not however in looking at patent machines, which were not very remarkable, but at the best and most interesting and complete collection from the South Sea islands that I ever saw. Arms, dress, tools, fishing hooks and nets, manufactures of cloth from the bark of trees, mats; I was very much interested. There were besides very interesting collections from the Indians of the west coast of N. America — Oregon, California, etc. In addition, I saw with much pleasure some of the most precious relics which America possesses. Personal relics of Washington: the suit he wore when relinquishing his commission, his camp equipage, sword, the original commission issued to him by the revolutionary congress; and the original Declaration of Independence, which I read from beginning to end. It is carefully framed and glazed and preserved in a glass case, Washington's sword standing at one side of it and a handsome gold-headed stick which belonged to Ben Franklin at the other — very appropriate supporters to such a shield. Washington's camp equipage contained among things a copper tea urn, a copper

kettle handsomely chased, and a copper coffee pot chased with a small oil or spirit lamp under it.

From this went again to the Capitol. Should say something of impressions of this building. Was much struck particularly yesterday when first saw it from some distance with its commanding position and imposing appearance on a hill, which raised it considerably above the greater part of the city. Immense flight of steps at the front . . . The Rotunda or large central hall with its fine cupola is very grand and imposing.

The large paintings round the walls are very interesting as they contain portraits of many interesting persons — tho' as works of art they are nothing particular. About the best of them is the baptism of Pocahontas. She is represented not so handsome as I had expected but with a girlish timid expression. She has a very good face however and her eyes, tho' nearly closed, you can see are fine. Her brother, who is present in the full costume of an Indian chief with an eagle in full plumage for his head-dress, is a noble-looking young man. The other paintings are: the Declaration of Independence, surrender of Burgoyne at Saratoga, of Cornwallis[38], and Washington surrendering his commission at Annapolis . . . [*reiterates he finds senators more impressive than congressmen, c. 100 words*]

Sunday [25 February]
After breakfast went to look for chapel. After some search met jolly old fellow, who when I asked if he could direct me civilly offered to show one to me as he was going that way. Praised Catholics and Irishmen. Spoke of Lent and fasting as a mark of sincerity. Observed pathetically: 'I haint got no religion myself.' Spoke highly of Gen. Shiels [James Shields] and said he met him yesterday looking well. Found I was an hour too soon for Mass. Walked back — went in to HG; made him understand more clearly my wishes about engineering, that merely wanted to learn. He said something about going as a volunteer.

Asked him if he could tell me anything about Mrs [Matilda] Tone or give me an introduction. [He replied:] 'Never go into society, know no

woman but my wife.' He seemed to be as busy as ever writing away.
Showed me paper — some interesting account about Col. Freemont[39].
Told me a Mr Fitman, a saddler, could give me information about any-
thing Irish and possibly about Mrs Tone.

Went to Mass at 11 o'c. Long low poor sort of chapel, something
like a country chapel in Ireland. Congregation of a poorer class tho'
comfortable. About one-fifth of the congregation Negroes, men and
women, boys and girls; most of them, as a decent Irishman next to me
said, slaves. They seemed devout and well behaved. I am told that
nearly all the blacks here — they are pretty numerous, most of the cab
drivers, etc., being so — are slaves. It seems to me that in general they
are less intellectual looking than the free blacks of NY. They have a
quiet submissive manner; some it seems to me dejected, tho' many, as
the cab drivers, are merry enough and laugh and joke together. Their
dress is much the same as that of any other labouring people according
to their occupation. I have seen some driving country carts and wagons;
they are poor looking, dejected creatures enough. I heard the masters
of some of them shouting in a rude authoritative manner, which you
never hear adopted towards a freeman in this country.

Towards evening, after a good read of [John] Milner[40], took a pretty
long walk towards the outskirts of the city, which are ragged enough,
hoping to come round to the north-west front of the Pres[idential]
House. Came to a pretty little Catholic Church. Vespers just over, heard
excellent preliminary discourse to a series of controversy. A good deal of
it same as Milner, but very well expressed and delivered [by a] fine young
priest, son of an Irishman name[d] Donnelan. Coming out pocket picked
of new silk handkerchief, for which I was fool enough some weeks ago at
NY to give 80 cents. Searched church and enquired, all in vain. Many
very respectable nice-looking people there; Catholics, also many
strangers — my friend the pickpocket as I hope among their number.

Monday [26 February]
Spent day between Supreme Court and Senate. Hoped to hear Webster
in former, as he was engaged to speak in a case about fraudulent sale of

lands in Maine by auction. Heard him, however, two or three times in Senate. Returned to Senate in the evening after dinner. Heard [William Rufus] King of Alabama, very gentlemany sensible man, who had been minister either in Paris or London. Also saw Hannigan [Edward Allen Hannegan], who is a little man, high cheekbones something like Dr Grey [John Gray][41], but I think a good face and, tho' plain looking, intelligent. Heard Berrin [John Macpherson Berrien], pleasing clever man, modest and unassuming in manner, rather Irish face and accent; expression of face rather like Mr Kenyon[42]. Heard Webster again, observed now his sweep of manner and his confident imposing delivery, not unlike [Daniel] O'Connell; more elegant and speaks very like a gentlemany Irishman. I read before going to bed Trig[onometry] and Milner.

Tuesday [27 February]
Walked out to Navy yard, scarcely anything doing, no ship on the stocks. Saw man making wooden boxes to hold charged bombshells and keep them dry. Rather deserted looking place. Remarked on my way the civility of people here. A man driving a wagon, of whom I asked the way, stopped, pointed it out and civilly offered me a seat — the same happened to me before. The soldier on guard at the gate was a civil Irishman.

Came back to the Supreme Court, found same man speaking still from yesterday — and Webster had not spoken yet. Should mention that yesterday were pointed out to me: C[hief] Justice Taney, Judges McLaine and Underwood. Judges generally very respectable-looking men, one of them very like Judge Ball[43] except his nose, which was a very handsome one. McLaine of Ohio a fine-looking man; the court very solemn and respectable; nine judges. Went into gallery of Senate. Heard Calhoun speak for five or ten minutes on question of extending time during which a patent may be renewed after it has expired to three years. He was against it. Hard sharp quick manner of speaking and accent like an Irishman.

Read and wrote journal and Trigonometry till 8 o'c. after dinner and then went up to the Senate. Heard rather interesting debate on the question of the purchase of [George] Catlin's[44] pictures by the State. Webster spoke very pleasing and wittily in favour — also Berrien — and lost.

In the morning enquired at church for handkerchief. Civil Irish sexton from Tyrone helped me to search to no purpose. Saw police magistrate over door, went in, was told great numbers of pickpockets here. One at least at each of the chief hotels and known to be so, so I was glad not to be at any of them. . . .

[*Alone in Washington except for Greeley, 'who is a mere acquaintance tho' a civil one' and a busy editor, Hart reflects on education and melancholy. He is opposed to boarding schools because they tend 'to weaken that sort of perfect affection and confidence which should exist between parent and child'. On the other hand, the character of an older person can be strengthened by separation from home and friends: 'For a day or two I sometimes felt a little downcast and lonely. However, I found that by stoutly resisting this feeling it shortly disappeared altogether, and while it was disappearing the idea occurred to my mind that this was certainly a useful exercise and could not fail to be very advantageous to me for the rest of my life.' C. 700 words.*]

Wednesday, 28 February
Spent morning till 1 o'c. reading Trig. and writing journal. Went to Senate and Supreme Court for a little. Wrote again after dinner. Wrote and read Mahan[45] till time to go to Levee. HG, who had promised to come with me, not being returned from the Capitol went up alone. Left my coat and hat with black in the hall and walked thro' in the crowd. Great many persons there but not half the number that came afterwards. Inferior military band playing in the hall, whole scene rather disorderly. People generally carelessly dressed, many shabbily; ladies badly dressed . . . the majority in full dress, others in ordinary dress, some even with bonnets. All sorts of people seemed to come in, there was no exclusion. I saw even some lads with dirty boots and clothes walking thro' like the rest.

Passed from the hall thro' one small room into another where President Polk stood, one or two gentlemen about him. He stood pretty nearly between the two doors, thro' one of which the stream of people entered and thro' the other of which they went out. He stood as it were on the right bank of the stream and shook hands and said 'How do you do, Sir,' to all or most of those who passed, myself among the number. We passed along one side of the room. Behind him in the room were numbers of ladies and officers in handsome blue uniform, some naval and some military, and some in citizens' dress.

Pres. Polk much older looking man than I had expected. Seemed feeble, rather plain, quiet looking; seemed rather passive and anxious to be polite; has something of a Northern face — sufficiently intelligent but more of a painstaking hardworking look. Would have taken him for some kind of student or great book-reader from his look — his eyes are rather small but bright and deep-set. On the whole he gave me the impression of a man much worn and exhausted by the fatigues of office.

Passed thro' and in the next room, a fine large one, stood aside to look at the people as they passed. Must say the ladies present, with one or two exceptions, gave a very unfavourable impression of American beauty. I think however they were anything but a select assemblage. Saw the venerable Mrs [James] Madison. Must have been a fine looking woman; is still strong and healthy looking and quite erect. Saw [James] Buchanan: fine commanding able-looking man. Saw Gen. Cass: very large man, shrewd able-looking fellow. Went around in the stream to see Mrs Polk, whom I had not seen before. Ladylike looking woman; not very handsome, seems a good deal younger than he is; something about her mouth and teeth reminded me of Mrs H[enry] O'H[ara].[46] Saw Commodore [Foxhall] Parker. Waited to see Gen. Shields but could not. Nobody seemed very particular about dress, clean gloves or gloves at all in many instances — neither ladies [n]or gentlemen.

Thursday [1 March]
Have just been speaking to HG. Advises me to wait till after Monday, the day of the inauguration. Think this is not unreasonable but will not quite make up my mind till tomorrow morning, as hope then to get letters from NY enclosing mine from Europe, which I am surprised and

annoyed not to have got before now as I know the *Europa* has been at NY for nearly a week. Can only account for the delay on the supposition that they have been sent first to JD, whom I imagine is at Albany.

Wrote part of letter home. Between 12 o'c. and 2 [p.m.] went up to Willard's Hotel to see Gen. Taylor, who receives during that time every day. Asked the way to his room and was shown it and walked up without ceremony. Found him in a small room about half-filled with gentlemen and a few ladies. Knew him at once in the midst of the crowd from his pictures. Seemed rather bewildered by the number of persons he had to receive. Manner not very dignified but good-natured. Heard him say just after I went in: 'Glad to see you, General, remember you were one of our council of war, always glad to meet you here or on the field of battle.' Heard him begin to praise or pass some compliment on a state, supposing it to be this state from which someone who was introduced to him came. The person corrected him saying, 'Kentucky, General,' — 'Oh, Kentucky is it?'

And asked a man near me to introduce me when old Zach was approaching. He overheard me, shook me warmly by the hand, saying out quite loud: 'Introduce yourselves, gentlemen, introduce yourselves, I am in your hands.' While he was saying this to me and the rest I had a longer shake than the others. I rather felt for him as the forefinger of his right hand was tied up as if it were cut, which must have made shaking hands unpleasant enough. His accent is plain and simple and rather like that of a north of Ireland farmer. His face is more good-natured looking than his likenesses represent it, and I would say that he is a good kind man. In battle he no doubt had the stern look his likenesses give him. Dressed in a blue frock coat — civilian's dress. His daughter, Mrs Bliss, was present receiving ladies, a few of whom [were] nice looking and nicely dressed. She is a very clever looking young lady and seemed very agreeable and cheerful.

After dinner went out in stage[coach] to Georgetown to see the Catholic College, of which I had read in my guide book, having first walked up to the Capitol [and] looked in to the Senate and Supreme Court. After some few inquiries found the college; met four or five of the students standing at the gate. Asked one of them if strangers were permitted to see the college. He answered me most politely; told me to go up to the hall door and that any of the prefects would be very happy to show me round. Went up, met at door very nice little boy about fourteen or fifteen coming out with his father. Offered at once most politely to find someone to show me round.

Meantime, his father and I entered into conversation in the parlour. Told me he had been a Quaker and a native of Philadelphia or its neighbourhood — had become a convert [to Roman Catholicism]. His eldest son, a very fine young man, had been educated here and had finally joined the establishment, which he told me was a Jesuit one. And that he would not be surprised if this little fellow would also join when he was old enough. Nice little boy came back and told me that one of the fathers would soon be disengaged. Thanked him and remained looking at the prints, among which was a fine large one of O'Connell.

After some time two lads, seventeen or eighteen years of age, looked in and, seeing a stranger, politely came forward and finding that I had not got anyone to show me round offered to do so themselves. They got the keys and showed me their museum, fine library, chapel, study room, remarkably fine refectory and dormitories, from which latter there is a noble view of the surrounding country, the Potomac river, the city of Washington. And the college is beautifully situated high and in a fine undulating rather hilly country, very favourable for exercise walking. No deaths have ever occurred, they told me, among the students and sickness is almost unknown. Number of student boarders at present is eighty-five, which they consider rather small. There are also day scholars. They pointed out to me from the top windows a vast extent of land belonging to the college and a fine vineyard near the house, from which to make all the wine they required. . . There are also farms attached to the college.

One of my conductors was a nice slight bright-eyed lad from Maryland named Hamilton, a Catholic, the other much to my surprise was a Protestant. He told me that there were about twenty Protestant boarders. They go to Mass like the rest, a good many of them become

Catholics afterwards. I was much pleased with the gentlemany frank natural manner of these boys, their politeness in coming forward, etc. I thought that their conduct and indeed also the demeanour of the other boys whom I met here contrasted favourably with what I have seen exhibited at other schools. There was a gentlemany ease and freedom from all shyness and awkwardness and, on the other hand, instead of rudeness or boorishness or tittering, a politeness and real anxiety to please. I even felt somewhat affected I was so gratified to find all this. We parted very good friends. I gave them my card and went back to Washington much pleased at my trip. Wrote part of letter home. Read Trig. and Milner — went for a little to Senate.

Friday, 2 March
Wrote home. Went to Senate and Supreme Court, where expected to hear Webster reply in a case that had been going for whole week. Found after watching for some time that would not. Heard Calhoun speak in the Senate — hard sharp quick accent and delivery. Graceful gesture leaves the impress of sincerity, which his antagonist Webster does not.

After dinner about 4 o'c. got a letter from MO'F from NY, enclosing an introduction to Mrs Tone from Richard Emmet. Went to enquire immediately of a man whom HG said knew everything Irish — her residence was not mentioned in the letter — he was out. Sat up very late writing my letter home as I determined to post it on Saturday. . .

Saturday, 3 March
Got up pretty early, finished my letter and wrote one to MO'F. Dressed and went out at 12 to breakfast. Enquired again for Mrs Tone's but found the man, Mr Fitman, a saddler, out again, but heard she lived at Georgetown. Ascertained at Coleman's Hotel that would find out anyone at Georgetown by asking at the Union Hotel, as there was no directory published. Went out. Owner of the Union Hotel directed me most politely. Found the house, a fine one tho' now somewhat neglected. Found that Mrs T. was not well, had a cold and was not able to be up but very kindly expressed a wish to see me some other time. Promised

to call again on Monday evening. Walked back and down to where the boats [start] for Alexandria. Have ascertained that boat started at nine in the morning. Determined to be up early, hear Mass and go down by boat and out to see Mount Vernon[47].

Read and after dinner for some time went up to Senate. Found the crowd very great, got in a short way and heard Webster make a short but interesting and vehement speech. Crush and heat was so tremendous came away soon, after trying vainly at both doors to get anything of a good place. Went to bed early, having first ascertained that there was to be Mass at 7.30 in the morning.

Sunday, 4 March
Up in good time [to] hear Mass. Down to boat, a couple of miles walk. . . Down to Alexandria, down the Potomac, fine river, beautiful morning. Breakfast at an oyster house, frightful coffee, never tasted such stuff in my life; fine oysters, overcharged. Hired a buggy with some difficulty. Started off with favourable gales and a serene silky Negro slave boy sitting beside me, driving capital horses and light vehicle. Would have got on admirably but the roads were *horrible*. Nothing like them I do believe in the whole world, sometimes in beds of rivers, sometimes nearly sunk in quicksands.

Country in summer or spring must be very beautiful and my black friend said it is so. Fine undulating country. Well wooded here and there. This part of Virginia and the adjacent part of Maryland about Washington are very similar, all of this undulating character. After passing thro' a country for some distance, which was cultivated and laid out in fields, neat farmhouses and even one or two gentlemen's places here and there, came to a wilder part of the country. The road quite a path thro' the woods; in no place did it seem to be made, but here it had still less appearance of being beaten down. We frequently in preference drove on the grass and over small shrubs and underwood.

Came at last to a more open cheerful sort of wood with this rude sort of road running thro' it. Saw several Buzzards floating along over my head. Negro told me they are respected and never shot or interfered with in any way. He also showed me several mocking birds — they do not begin to sing till the middle of the month — also snow birds, blue birds, etc. Told me wild turkeys very plenty here but did not see any. Shortly told me we were now in the lands of Mount Vernon. The present owners have sold off a good deal; the estate still contains 2,000 acres, all in the hands of the owner. To the left there was a vast extent towards the river, where maize had been grown last year; the stumps of straw were still standing a foot or a foot and a half over the ground as is common in this country.

At last we came to the gates and on entering found, strange to say, that all we had yet encountered in the way of bad roads was nothing to the avenue. It beat all I ever saw. The house is pretty and beautifully situated, surrounded by an undulating finely-wooded country, high over the river close to it and commanding a very fine view of it. A lawn of some size stretches in front of the house towards the river and there is then a steep almost perpendicular descent, thickly covered with trees, running down nearly to the water's edge.

I walked down to see his [Washington's] tomb. I can easily understand how he was attached to this place. I think one could live very happily in it: the calm, the fine view, the beautiful woods — the wild birds, the wild deer, of which there were great numbers at one time not far from our road. It must be a delightful place. Disappointed at not being admitted into the house. Present owner, Capt. Washington — a grandnephew of George Washington — curious sort of man I was told.

Started for home. On the road both going and returning thought how Washington had passed along that road frequently, even at the time when the fate of this country was still very uncertain, perhaps at the very time when he was first called from Mount Vernon to command the armies of the Continental Congress. On way back cut a grapevine with some difficulty as a relic. Think it was within the limits of Mnt. Vernon, at all events very near. Hope I shall make a good stick of it but fear not.

Found Negro very intelligent. Surprised one much, saluted his acquaintances, black and even some white, with a great deal of readiness and bonhomie. Declared he was very happy as he was raised in the family and was treated like one of themselves. Knew the distance of Richmond, Virginia, all the birds, trees, etc. Drew up at one farmhouse, called to a slave for a glass of water and handed him a tip or 5-cent piece. Then pulled out a large silver watch before starting. Most attentive and civil, tucking in Buffalo robe. (Remarked that reason Buffalo robe or hide so warm a covering is that besides the hair there is close to the skin a thick short coat of wool or fur.) I observed a greater freedom and independence of manner than would be exhibited by an Irish or even an English servant in similar circumstances. Whenever I did not choose to talk, which however he seemed to like, he sang to amuse himself. . . Had altogether an independent and self-reliant way about him.

Came back to Washington in steamboat, which luckily for me touched at Alexandria. While standing on the jetty was hailed as 'stranger' by an Irishman evidently long in America, who told me what an odd man Capt. Washington was; told me he himself was in the grocery business and supplied Mnt. V. (Irishmen everywhere). Read a little and went to bed early. Remember[ed] Nigger; when asked what sort of man the present owner of Mnt. V. was, shrugged his shoulders and said: 'You look at the place, sir, and you can tell what sort of man he is' — with a degree of readiness and shrewdness which surprised me.

Monday, 5 March 1849
After consulting HG, by his advice determined to remain in my room till Old Jack came up and then to go alongside him to the Capitol; 12 o'c. procession came on, several companies of volunteers in very becoming uniforms and marching in excellent style; and at last Old Jack in an open carriage with Ex-Pres. Polk, Fullamore [Millard Fillmore][48] and the Mayor. OJ bowing with the most agreeable face on all sides. The windows everywhere in P[hiladelphi]a Avenue were for long before crowded with ladies, who waved handkerchiefs as he passed. I liked his face and general appearance much better than I had supposed from his pictures.

Made my way to the rear of the Capitol and got a good place among the crowd in front of the platform. On it were two red velvet armchairs and a few benches and chairs of black haircloth ranged behind. After some delays, the drawing up of the volunteers in front of the platform, Old Jack appeared with Chief Justice Taney and followed by a crowd of Senators, Pres. Polk, the foreign ambassadors, etc. He, after bowing to the cheers of the crowd, sat down rather sideways on his chair and pulling out his handkerchief and spectacles carefully wiped the latter and stuck them upon his forehead.

After a time he and Judge Taney, who in the meantime had sat down in the other red chair, rose and OJ took the Oath on the Testament administered by Taney. He then pulled out a couple of sheets of letter paper and read his address, of which I could hear scarcely any except towards the end when he raised his voice and turned more towards the people. Both the taking of the oath and the end of his speech were hailed by the shouts of the people and the roar of cannon. When he was done numbers of those about him on the platform shook hands warmly with him. Among the first to do so was Polk, with his grave sedate manner. He had sat all the time in his cloak and hat and long grey hair, looking very grave and contented and seemed to me a more intellectual looking man than I had thought him at his Levees.

After bowing for some moments all round to the people, Old Jack put on a sort of military cloak and made his way back thro' the crowd, most of whom remained to gaze upon the crowd below, volunteers, etc. Soon after he came out, as I think at the side or private entrance to the Supreme Court, and got into his carriage with Polk and drove quickly away. I was much impressed with the whole scene — with its simplicity and common sense — backed . . . by the unanimity and intelligence of the people and by military force if necessary as the cannon and above all the presence of Old Jack [and] Gen. Scott, with Mexican and other recollections, reminded you.

While walking about I met the ambassadors and their wives going away. I thought that they seemed out of place in their fine uniforms and altogether they did not seem in their element. No doubt there were many American uniforms to be seen but they were practical and intended for use and not merely to form part of a pageant, which those

were. Came away more impressed than ever with the marked differ-
ences between this and European countries, from the highest to the
lowest, and understanding as I think still better the feelings with which
Americans must regard many things in the older countries. I also
thought that ambassadors and enlightened men, who had seen something of this country and its institutions, must have a very different idea
of it from what is instilled into the Masses in Europe and must look
down on the Masses when they return as inferior and blind; but that it
is better that things should be as they are for a certain class, and that for
the country (England, for instance) generally the evils of any funda-
mental change would far more counter-balance any advantage from a
more rational or liberal system.

In this immense crowd, as generally in all in this country, it is very
remarkable that everyone seems to be dressed in good cloth clothes. On
railroads, etc., you see men in working clothes, but on festivals each of
those men is dressed in good broadcloth, and on all occasions those
whose occupations are anything except rude manual labourers dress in
good cloth clothes. In this part of the country cloaks are the usual garment
and everyone almost seemed to have a cloak. It is not so more north in
NY, tho' even there they are more worn than in Ireland or England. . .

After the inauguration of Gen. Taylor as President, I walked out to
Georgetown hoping to see Mrs W[olfe] Tone, having left my introduction from Richard Emmet on Saturday previous. . . Was shown up to
the Library, a comfortable room with bookshelves well filled all round.
Her attendant at first expressed some fears that she would not be able
to see me but said she would try. Saw Mrs T. Her memory failed a little
sometimes about recent events, but about anything that happened long
ago she was as clear and bright as possible. She chatted very gaily, spoke
with great feeling and affection about Ireland — of the 'College' [Trin-
ity College, Dublin], of Dr Whitley Stokes[49], who she said was 'not a
friend but a brother'.

Said 'I lived twenty years in France and am almost a Frenchwoman'.
Spoke of the Bonapartes. Said 'Lucien[50] was the very best of them', 'he
was the beauty of the family'. When I said he must have been very

handsome if he were handsomer than Napoleon, [she replied] 'Napoleon certainly had a beautiful Grecian face, but Lucien was taller and better figure.' Told laughingly and in an animated, pleasing manner the story of Napoleon's sending his brother Jerome, who was a boy of fifteen or sixteen when he was First Consul, to school to McDermot, an Irishman who kept the best school then in Paris[51]. Jerome was spoiled by the flattery of his companions, dressed extravagantly and ran into debt in various ways. Napoleon, hearing of this, came to school one day, boxed his ears soundly and made him take off his fine clothes and put on very plain coarse ones and sentenced him to wear them till he had given satisfactory proofs of his attention to his studies by getting a good place in his class. This however did not do him much good. Being the brother of the First Consul and a 'pretty boy' he was much admired and flattered, which of course ruined him.

Asked frequently for 'poor old Dublin' and, when I told her how much it [had] fallen from its former prosperity, said 'I am sorry, very sorry for it'. She lived just opposite Anne Street in Grafton Street, close by [St] Ann's Church. Spoke of a 'beautiful little theatre that used to be kept up in Ship Street' . . . of a man of the name of Kane O'Hara[52], who was a great beau, used to dress in the old French style, wear a queue — who used to be the chief manager of this theatre in which many amateurs used to act, her brother [Edward] With[e]rington among the rest. When a child she used to be greatly afraid of this O'Hara. Said her father[53] was an Englishman when mentioning that her grandfather, Fanning[54], was a great friend of Sir Lucius O'Brien, a member of the Irish Parliament[55]. I said Mr Fanning was an MD.

I said that it was wonderful she had such strong Irish feeling. 'Ah', [she replied] in a rather sad voice, 'it was Tone gave it all to me.' She had shortly before mentioned his name when speaking of the College. She fully understood when I mentioned that the old wall had been taken down and railings put in its place. She observed that it must be a great improvement and said that she knew the College well and 'Tone was such a pet there. I used after I was married to walk constantly there and could go where I pleased, to the museum', etc.

Something being said about my remaining in this country, she said: 'Oh, don't expatriate yourself, don't expatriate yourself. Here I am for thirty years in this country and I have never had an easy hour, longing after my native land.' Either at this time or when speaking of Dublin, she said: 'I often thought of going back to see it once more but could not summon up courage and I suppose I shall never see it now.' Poor old lady she seemed very weak, tho' she chatted and asked questions with great animation for a long time. Nothing could be more ladylike than her manner and expressions and she must have had considerable powers of conversation.

Said of S[mith] O'B[rien], etc., that they were punished for what she called 'being virtuous' . Said of Ireland: 'I have been for the best part of my life, and I can tell you I am not very young, hoping and watching for something to turn up for that country, but I am afraid that now there is no hope, it's too small'; and after a pause, 'do you know, I sometimes wish it would grow'. Said about the amount of arms in Ireland that it was always exaggerated; that 'it is old ground to me, I have frequently seen them get in estimates which always proved the real amount to be very insignificant and to have been much exaggerated'. Said 'that about the year '98 the great obstacles were place-begging and dissensious [*sic*] religions and others, said that the former was naturally the result of slavery which deprived men of energy and made them look rather to government than to their own industry and exertions'.

Her face was rather square, a forehead rather broad than high tho' quite sufficiently so; straight and still at eighty years beautifully smooth and fair; nose straight, perhaps a little thick; under lip slightly projecting, eyes full of light, as was her whole face. Must have been very pretty and most attractive and ladylike in manner. Accent Irish, Dublin and pleasing. Came away much pleased and rather affected, feeling for the first time some idea of what poor TWT suffered for Ireland and what a heroine his wife was. Lived in fine old house in Georgetown.

[recte] 6 March
Started at 6 a.m. in train for Baltimore. A number of volunteers who

had come to the inauguration in train returning, were allowed to pass free of charge. Spent the day from 9 a.m. in Baltimore. Walked all thro' it; got on top of Washington Monument, a very handsome pillar. Thought Baltimore very beautiful city, parts of it reminded me of Hotwells Clifton. Thought for a short time that it was a pity that JD had not seen it before he settled in NY, but soon perceived that it was very inferior to it in trade and apparent wealth.

Large Irish quarter, good houses of a middling sort and streets kept clean; many foundries; Shot Tower, Catholic Cathedral and Bishop's Palace most prominent buildings in the city[56]. Cathedral large, interior rather gloomy, reminded me somewhat of Cathedral of Florence. Came away that evening in steamboat by Chesapeake to Newcastle, across Delaware to mouth of Delaware River, and so up to Philadelphia. Remarked in Baltimore very few Negroes, infinitely fewer than in Washington, where they are very numerous. In fact as it seemed to me they are in a majority there, tho' this I am told is far from being the case; and a moment's reflection shows me that they are a small minority. The first hasty impression was probably produced by the fact that a great many of the loungers in the streets, cab-drivers, porters, waiters, messengers, etc., being black, so that wherever you turn you seem to see black faces about you.

7 March

Landed at Philadelphia. After breakfast went out to see the city. Should mention that in the steamboat coming up the Delaware, in which I and the rest sat up or lay on the floor or tables all night, one man said that he had lost, been robbed of, a wallet or pocket book containing a considerable amount of money. After some debate, it was resolved to hold a public meeting on the subject and H. Greeley was voted into the chair. This was rather an American piece of business, the people taking into their own hands and troubling themselves about what elsewhere would have been left to the police, or not be attended to at all. It was proposed to appoint searchers and to search all on board. Various propositions and suggestions were made as to the mode of doing this;

some said that it was no use now, as they had been talking about it so much they had given the thief full notice and time to secrete it.

There was some confusion, some of those present were only half awake. In the confusion, and before any resolution had been come to, the loser and some others mistaking something that had been said, or conceiving that the resolution to search had been passed, proceeded to search a very respectable looking young gentleman, who seemed much surprised but consented to be searched at once. He was not the thief, however. Then either perceiving their mistake, or for some other cause, they proceeded no further; the meeting broke up without doing anything. Some time after, the elder brother of the young man searched, who had been asleep [and] who was a sea captain, heard that his brother had been searched and went immediately and made the loser come and make an apology. He explained his mistake by saying that at the time he thought he had been robbed, when paying his fare he remarked two or three men with white top coats near him and this young man had a white top coat.

During the night a man called a baggage master came round with a tin box with slits in it like that in a poor box, each slit large enough to let pass one of the baggage checks. At each slit was written the name of one of the hotels in Philadelphia, or of the railroads. Anyone who chose gave him his check, mentioning at the same time the hotel at which you meant to stop, or if you were going thro' by any of the railroads. He put your check into the corresponding slit thro' which it fell into its proper compartment in the box. I gave him mine and, on arriving at Philadelphia, went straight to the hotel I had mentioned, got breakfast, went out to see the town without taking any trouble about my trunk, except merely telling them about it at the hotel and requesting them to pay the 26 cents which was his regular charge. By this means I saved about an hour and a great deal of trouble watching and waiting, and then employing someone at perhaps double the expense to carry it up. He having a great many, and putting them all into a large van, is able to do it more cheaply and expeditiously.

Went to Independence Hall and then stood in the doorway looking out on the park from which the Declaration was read to the People. Impressive enough to be walking about as it were in the very footprints of those remarkable men, who on that occasion so boldly and with such dignity defied the power of England and threw off her yoke.

Went out to see Gerard College. The central building, containing lecture rooms chiefly, is very beautiful, reminding one somewhat of the Madeleine at Paris but not so imposing or beautiful. It is built of white marble. Whether it was that the day was gloomy or the place unfinished, but something about it reminded [me] continually of an eccentric hard old man, which impression the full-length statue in the hall was not calculated to remove. Without wishing to be uncharitable, I could not help feeling that there was a degree of egotism and display about and a sort of caprice in some of the rules not allowing carriages inside the enclosure, etc. Tried to see the mint but could not get in. From whatever reason did not much like Philadelphia — certainly the weather was not favourable. Crossed to Camden in a ferry, and came in railroad to Ambay and from that to N. York by water, passing along a good deal of coast of Staten Island.

Thought N. York looked a great and fine city and that the harbour, shipping, etc., exceeded anything I had seen a thousand-fold. Felt almost like coming home and drove [down] old familiar gay Broadway in excellent spirits. Found JD and MO'F in 541 Houston St. and heard all the details of JD's admission to the Bar. Determined to remain in NY till after Easter, as Lent a bad time for travelling.

Employed time from 7 March to 29 April reading Macaulay's *History of England*, 1st and 2nd vols.; Tucker's *Life of Thomas Jefferson*, 2 vols.; Marshall's *Life of Washington*, 5 vols., together with some engineering and trigonometry; finishing Milner's *End of Contriving*; reading the greater part of the N. Testament and some of the Old; writing Journal and letters, etc.

15 April [1849][57]

. . . [R]eflecting on the horrors of revolution and civil war — and thinking how natural it is for those who take an interest in industrial pursuits or commerce or possess property to abhor those who are disposed to bring war and strife, chance of plunder and spoliation to their doors — and also feeling how happy a thing it is to live in a country where it is not necessary to engage in political revolutionary struggles or projects. I have found it difficult to recall the precise state of feeling in which my mind, and I have no doubt that of many others, was previous to the late attempt in Ireland, and also to account for that strong feeling of the probability of success — the disregard of what may now seem to be the necessary elements of success, which a more accurate knowledge of this country and of its struggle induced the mind to think indispensable. Also to account for that blind confidence in the inherent strength and fury of the people, vague idea that arms would not be wanting, etc., but would be forthcoming.

On reading today the reprint in the *People* of Reilly's article, 'The Sicilian Fashion' [*sic*][58], the whole tide of feeling came back again to my mind: the strong parallel between the supposed condition of Sicily and the Sicilians and Ireland, also between the Irish and the inhabitants of Milan, both supposed to be trodden down, degraded as far as it was possible to do and known to be disarmed, beset with spies and police and opposed by a powerful military force. In some degree, too, the examples of Paris, Milan, Berlin, where, tho' the people were more military and intelligent, their attempts followed by such remarkable successes seemed to be impulsive and without organisation. All these remarkable occurrences conduced to the belief that there was going on thro' the world a general upheaving of suffering and downtrodden people, however previously humbled and broken-spirited they were.

The desperate evils which afflicted Ireland seemed not alone to equal but far to exceed any suffered by those peoples that had risen and fought with such desperation, and it seemed not unlikely that on their 'own hook' and without 'Leaders' they would attempt something instigated by their sufferings and the examples of others. If to this be added the accounts given by various enthusiastic, or possibly not veracious, people of the high spirits and dispositions of the country people, the visible excitement and the loud speaking and the arming to a great degree in the towns — and also the generally believed at least partial disaffection of the troops evinced in many ways, their fighting with their more loyal comrades, letters said to have been written by them, shouting for Repeal, it is said, treating some of the more known leaders with marks of respect, etc.

All this, coupled with the exciting and able writing of the poets, journalists — with all there was a great degree of enthusiasm and a sort of emulation of the brave deeds of the heroes of Palermo, Paris, Milan, etc., which probably strongly influenced the mind to overlook or disregard obstacles and to imagine the people to have those feelings, to be in that state in which one wished them to be. [Other factors were] the spirit of Patriotism so carefully fostered by the journals and the strong conviction that it was now or never, that any spirit which remained in the country would be starved out of it in one more famine and all confidence in the leaders lost. Also that anything but force was not to be relied on, that voting by elections was nonsense on account of the corruption of the upper and middle classes, in whose hands the representation was.

One is rather disposed here in America, looking back at the whole affair, to wonder how people could be so deluded, seeing that the result has proved so contemptible. It is necessary, however, to take the above facts into consideration in order to form a just idea of the subject. In a country as the American colonies even — in which the people themselves possess a considerable degree of liberty, *a fair representation* and general prosperity and comfort, at least a fair share of it, cautious and moderate and just opposition to incipient oppression is necessary in order to carry the feelings and consent of the people with it; and to bring them step by step to that point where a recourse to arms becomes necessary, it is necessary to keep the oppressor in the wrong, to exhaust all peaceable means of asserting rights and to make him in every instance and in the last resort the aggressor.

In the case of Ireland, however, afflicted by the sharpest and most pressing evils, famine and pestilence, the food which would more than suffice for all the people dragged away and none brought to supply its place; oppressive rents and taxes exacted with the utmost rigour and cruelty, their houses torn down, and all this with a hostile parliament, in which they had no power or influence, and which signalised itself by oppressive measures, coercion bills, etc., ruling their destinies — it was not unnatural to suppose that no great time or management would be necessary to convince such a people to assert their rights, the rights of life and food, by fighting; nor to suppose that to talk to them of peaceful struggles and patience and putting their enemy in the wrong would seem very like cowardice and humbug — these also should be taken in connexion with the above remarks on the peculiar state of Europe.

It is not unnatural to feel on reading such an article as 'Sicilian Fashion' a sort of passion for taking a part in such scenes and fighting even a desperate battle for a good cause, and at the same time to feel a contempt for the peaceful pursuits of life — pursuing profession, trade, etc. A good deal of this however is only the poetry of the thing, the reality is very different. It is no doubt a glorious thing to fight for one's native land, or for any other if the occasion comes legitimately in one's way. A man should do it bravely if it comes before him, but in the meantime labour and toil to earn support is the lot of man imposed by his Creator, and tho' it may seem at times tame and shabby as compared with martial or patriotic exploits, it is nevertheless to be gone thro' just as we must eat to live. It may be absurd to note this as the general tendency is rather to attach too much importance to the matter of making money, living, eating, drinking, etc. — which I am not sure is not my own favourite side of the question after all.

I mean by this that many cannot understand the idea of a person risking health or life for anything in the world — that the answer 'but I might be killed or hanged or lose my property, etc.,' settles the question at once in any case whatever. Not so Washington, with his happy domestic habits and fine estates. Not so Wolfe Tone, with his youth, talents and unrivalled domestic happiness; not so *his wife*; not so Robert Emmet or Lord Edward [Fitzgerald]. Not so W. S. O'Brien or John Mitchel. Not so all who have devoted themselves for the good of others and who have held the gratification of living comfortably and quietly all their lives as contemptible, when compared with that of serving and elevating the human race, or that portion of it with which they were more immediately connected.

31 April

Determined after Easter to go out for some time to Mr Thomas Emmet[59], to try my hand at engineering, to see what kind of life it is. Was anxious that JD should have an office and be settled before I should go as then we should probably give up present rooms, as terms were reasonable only by three having them together. On account of the sitting room delayed from day to day; and then TE came to town to see his mother, who was very ill; then of course I could not go. Finally resolved that JD, MO'F and I should go up the North River for day or two, before he entered his office which he was to do on May 3rd or 4th.

Started on 30 April in *Isaac Newton*, magnificent boat, intending to stop at W. Point. But when we were about half way were told by Judge Harris[60], who was going up, that it did not stop till it got to Albany — so had to go on all night. Breakfasted at Albany and returned afterwards to W. Point. JD delighted, examined the forts, Putnam on the hill and Clinton below. Spoke to some of the cadets, a fine body of lads. Went thro' Library and in another building saw the drawing room of the cadets, and in it a likeness of André — giving the idea of an elegant, accomplished but rather weak man.

In the evening of Tuesday met at the hotel a nice handsome young officer, with whom JD entered into conversation. MO'F and I joined in soon after. We were much pleased with his frank and gentlemany, and at the same time modest and unassuming, deportment. He had been educated there and was spending part of his leave of absence there. He had been in Mexico and gave a very interesting account of some of the battles under Gen. Scott.

He was from S. Carolina, had a devoted admiration for J. C. Calhoun; and also of England, of her power and greatness, but seemed rather ignorant of her real situation, being dazzled by her achievements.

The American officers' undress uniform is in my mind very becoming: a white waistcoat and blue frock, with standing collar gold; a becoming blue cloth cap with gold eagle in front; trousers light grey or dark blue. There is a pretty painting in the church by Mr Muir, the teacher of the cadets, with the inscription: 'Righteousness exalteth a nation — but Sin is a disgrace to our people.'

Wednesday, 2 May
After seeing the forts, etc., and dining came away in steamer that passed at 2 o'c. MO'F and I stopped at Caldwell's Landing, ten or twelve miles farther down the river, and JD went on to N. York being anxious to see about [his law office]. (Before going farther must note that in the *Isaac Newton* coming up JD met Judge Harris, who took so kind and active a part in having him admitted to the Bar. I had a good opportunity of seeing and hearing him speak. I was much pleased with his very gentlemany, elegant appearance and manner. I don't know on the bench in Ireland a more, or indeed so, gentlemany and nice man in every way — in appearance, dress, etc. He was quite like an English or Irish gentleman of rank or an eminent lawyer, and after all those classes are the people of all the world whose appearance is generally most respectable and gentlemany. There is something always more free and easy about the American, which possibly after all is to be desired, and when he turns out as a regular dandy he does not to my taste do it at all as well as the English or Irishman. There is a French feeble effeminate style, which we are rather accustomed to associate with the idea of a hairdresser or dancing master.)

At Caldwell's Landing we found a pretty good sort of inn in which we determined to stop and, depositing our baggage, crossed over in a small boat to Peek Hill [*recte* Peekskill] and walked a considerable way up the country on the east side of the river. Was told that Paulding, one of those who took André, lived not far from Peekskill . . . his monument is not far from the village. Got our supper in regular Yankee fashion, with the woman of the house and one or two other people. Rough looking enough viands, pretty good.

3 May

Next morning up early, breakfast, and set off before 8 o'c. to walk
south along the western shore on which Caldwell's is situated. The road
goes close to the river, in some places high above it. The river is here
from a mile to a mile and a half wide, and presents the appearance of a
fine lake some four or five miles long. High mountains on the north and
west. Came at last to Stony Point and, after some scrambling, got out
to the extreme point of it and sat down for some time admiring the
view. Washed my hands in the Hudson at the extremity of Stony Point.
View from this very fine. You stand on a bold promontory and the river
presents the appearance of two lakes on each side, connected by the
narrower passage between Stony and Verplank points. Saw where on
the southern side of the point Gen. Wayne ('Mad Anthony' he was
called) came along the strand to surprise the fort. The present light-
house stands on the site of the fort.

Came back [to] the mainland and got old David Teryick to row us
across. Met on the shore an old man who said his father had been at the
taking of the fort. Teryick was helped in rowing us over by a tall extraordinary drunken 'loafer', to whom he had just given something to
drink. Landed at Verplank's Point — dined there — had a chat with a
funny little man who said he had a farm near Croton; spoke of his musical enjoyments — musical society — also a debating society called the
Two Harriets, he said, from two young ladies who had formed part of
a picnic [group] to those hills some years ago.

Verplank, almost an island separated from the mainland by water
and by marshes, seems fertile; large house of Mrs Verplank in a prominent position; descendant of old Dutch settler, I believe. Our host
showed us a grapeshot found near the ruins of the fort which was close
to the landing. Got on the mainland by a low road leading thro' rather
swampy ground. Country a good deal broken and rocky; here and there
a good farmhouse, all however of rather a middling kind; saw one with
a very fine old orchard.

Walked thro' the country to Peekskill, passing under an arch of the
Hudson River railroad which comes out on the river at Peekskill.

Crossed over in ferry. About half a quarter of a mile to the north of Uncle Sam's is the spot where some suppose the celebrated Capt. Kidd, the pirate, sunk a ship filled with treasure. Companies have been formed, and a portion of the neighbouring shore purchased or leased, for the purpose of seeking this treasure. . . . [*details of expensive works, suspended due to lawsuit, c. 120 words.*] The people there seem to think that the whole affair is a humbug, and got up much as railways have been for the purpose of selling stock. It is said they drew up one cannon, but the boatmen say that it was first put there for the purpose of being found.

To the south of U. Sam's about one mile are extensive brick works. Great quantities are made with inconceivable rapidity by the aid of a steam engine. Blue clay and sand are found close at hand in alternate beds. They are thrown into . . . large hoppers, ground or mixed together, and pressed into the moulds by machinery worked by steam. The cases of bricks were taken out of the machine and carried to the drying-floor by men. Some of the machines, of which there were many, were worked by horses; in some the moulding was done by hand. A great many men are employed here, nearly all Irishmen.

After tea walked out, ascended to the mountain road overhanging the river and walked northwards. Beautiful view — steamboats passing below up and down the fine stream. Could not help [thinking] continually, now and whenever I contemplated the appearance, life and industry and prosperity about this fine river, how often Washington had crossed and recrossed it, and how hard he had worked to make it and the whole country what they are. Found pretty far up some small houses. Near them were two women milking cows, one a German, the other an Irishwoman. Told us the land belonged to a Mr Morgan and that they paid for their share of it rent to him. A little farther on met a regular old mountaineer, who said he was a Welshman and turned out to be the identical Mr Morgan.

Had 300 acres of land, part mountain and useful only for cutting wood for firing, hickory rods for making hoops for barrels, etc.; and some fit enough for agriculture — some bottom meadow on a level

with and at one time apparently covered by the river, which had formerly made a considerable elbow just here. Educates his children by
sending one to a minister some miles off, or by boarding someone such
as a clerk in a store out of place or health, or somebody of at least ordinary education but poor, or who is satisfied with humble accommodation in this wild mountain region during the winter. He stated that this
is commonly done by farmers in the country, who are well pleased to
do so in order to have their children taught.

He came from Glamorganshire in 1823, became rather affected in
speaking of the 'old country'. Asked if he ever felt sorry for [leaving]
it, [he replied:] 'It's no use speaking of that now.' Had a fine face and
eyes. When parting shook hands most warmly, having first invited us to
spend the night with him. When we told him we were Irishmen, said
we must be from some of the cities — 'for you speak English so well'.
He did not however imagine, as I at first supposed, that the majority of
the Irish spoke Irish, for he said: 'Your countryman who lives down
there speaks it very differently, quite broad.' He supposed that all, or
nearly all, in Ireland were like those he was accustomed to see.

I have observed that many such men, however shrewd and intelligent — even some men in business . . . are very ignorant as to the state
of other countries; which is after all but natural for those who have not
seen and had some opportunity to observe a few foreign countries, and
who have not had time or opportunity to read about them. At parting
he said: 'I do not know whether you are rich or poor, but whenever
you settle down on land or otherwise *be honest*, it's the best way in the
end.' There was something very impressive and earnest in his manner,
and there seemed to be a depth of feeling and reflection about him that
seems to be wanting generally in Americans. It may be their manner
which leaves this impression of the people you meet here in business:
'Be cautious, they're *great* rogues; they'll not rob you, but if they can
get $1,000 more or so out of you (using an expressive gesture) and be
called gentlemen afterwards, they'll do it.'

[*Hart inserted a note on 21 May displaying his gullibility:*] Heard since
from MO'F, who spent a week at Caldwell's, that our old philosopher

is a regular old pirate and cuts down other people's wood besides his own, and with his gang of retainers is the terror of the neighbourhood in winter. Returning met an ill-looking Irishman who lived in a house beautifully situated near the river. Would not believe that we were Irishmen. When MO'F said he was a Connaughtman, said if he was he ought to be thrown down the rocks. Found out he was a rancorous Orangeman and one of the class called Fardowners. From this circumstance I strongly suspect that the division and feuds between Corkonians and Fardowners is really only a continuation of those between Orangemen and Catholics in the 'old country', and are not quite so unmeaning as I had previously supposed.

Friday, 4 May
Up early at 5 o'c., saw fine sunrise on the Hudson. Crossed over in boat to Peekskill to take steamer which started at 6 o'c. Sailed down and reached Sing Sing about 7 [a.m.], breakfasted and set off to walk up the country a little after 8. Sing Sing pretty place; country at first rather [flat?], then for six or seven miles in a direction NE from Sing Sing till one reached Pine Bridge, rugged and rather poor. Came to the Croton lake formed by damming up the Croton River. Skirted along it, crossed it at Pine Bridge and after about two miles more came to the Croton dam, a fine work at which the water enters the aqueduct.

Found a small inn kept by a jolly young host who told us he had 'burst up at N. York'; which did not seem to trouble him much; gave us a good dinner. When we told him that we were Irishmen, said his grandfather was one, that his name was McLaughlin and that somehow or other it had got transformed to Laflin, probably from the Yankees supposing that 'laugh' should be pronounced the same way in an Irish name as in the English verb or noun.

Walked back to S. Sing by a shorter way which made the distance about six miles — a good part of the way along the top of the embankment or mound like the embankment of a railway in which the aqueduct is contained. On our return saw some beautiful land and pretty houses. The views from different points very beautiful there in presenting the appearance of a number of lakes among hills, from its frequent windings and its great width. The formation of the Croton lake by the damming up of the Croton River has created quite a new feature in the country and changed its appearance. A stout old farmer we met at the inn said that just near Pine Bridge there was a fine farmhouse and thirty acres of as good land as there was in the country which is now covered by the water. Got home to Sing Sing pretty well tired, having walked about fifteen miles and the day being very warm.

Saturday, 5 May
Went after breakfast to see the great prison of Sing Sing. Were very civilly shown thro'; a clerk entering our names and residences in a book, for which 25 cents each was charged or 25 cents for the two I forget which. Nothing was expected or would be taken by the guard for his trouble. Saw prisoners at work at their various trades, which seems to be a most rational and human[e] mode of employing them. File making and carpet weaving are taught to those who are considered fit. Almost every other trade however is practised: stockings, hats, shoes, harness, etc.

Some are employed in the kitchen, some are hired out on the railroad works, at least that part of them which pass thro' the prison. The Hudson River railroad passes thro' the prison disfiguring it a good deal. When completed however it will be arched over and the effect will not be so bad. There is a separate building, higher up on the hill, for women; there were about sixty women. Some of them were employed in sewing, others covering buttons and their dress and appearance was neat and uniform. The whole place remarkably clean and neat. The number of men was about 700.

The guard told us that they generally contrived to give persons who had been in the better positions of life as merchants, etc., some of whom were there, such employment as attending the sick, they not being accustomed to labour. There were a great many coloured people here but far the majority, as is natural from the relative population, were white men. Guards with loaded guns were posted at different points on the heights and all about to prevent prisoners escaping — probably because opportunity was afforded by the breach and confusion made by the railroad.

A few hours after MO'F took a steamer going up the river to return to Caldwell's, I took a boat going down to go to Tarrytown. At the inn at Sing Sing there were a number of men, all I believe inspectors on the railroad. Their appearance, manner, etc., was by no means attractive; they seemed to me much about the same as a set of rowdy law clerks; they seemed to live and board there. This gave me rather a disgust to the engineering life, where very probably one would not be even so high as one of those, and should have them for associates. Think JD's idea a good one: 'That it is a mistake for one who can command some little money to enter on a pursuit in which anyone who has nothing but a pair of hands and a head and knows how to read and write can compete on equal terms.'

Soon reached Tarrytown. Engaged there a light one-horse wagon to take me thro' Sleepy Hollow, the scene of Ichabod Crane's adventures. Stopped at the spot where Major André was taken and saw where the great tree had stood, under which the three militia men were sitting playing cards when they first saw André watering his horse at a little stream which crosses the road. Sleepy Hollow a long narrow valley filled with farmhouses and orchards; went up to the old Dutch church; a young man who drove [by] pointed out Beckman's house, rendered remarkable by the heroic Mr Beckman. Strange feeling to be on the spot where that most interesting event, the capture of André, occurred; the very road by which he came still called the Turnpike road. . . Could almost imagine I saw him riding along, and carelessly and in security stopping to let his horse drink.

Felt much interest in viewing the scene of Washington Irving's *Legend of Sleepy Hollow*, which by the way is the real name of the valley. Remem[bered] to have been deeply interested by hearing it read by Revd Mr Burke long ago at school at Castleknock. Saw the gloomy hollow from which the Dominie stalwart rival started in the disguise of the headless Hessian. Little thought when at thirteen years of age

I listened to 'Father Michael' reading the story on English composition or on Elocution day I should ever see the scene, which at the time I regarded as a sort of mystic or fairy land so dreamily is it described by W. Irving.

Drove across to White Plains, about six miles, to take railroad to NY; my driver nice *gentlemany young* man, apparently the son of the innkeeper from whom I hired the wagon; intelligent and polite, pointed out everything of interest to me and stopped wherever it was desirable to do so. Day was very wet but with good umbrella and fine buffalo robe did not mind it. Got into NY about 7 p.m. at end of Houston St. and, bag in hand, walked up to Mrs Medhurst's. Country from Tarrytown to White Plains, and thence to N. York, rugged and not attractive. Passed in railroad a large building, with a great many large wooden crosses topping every peak and gable end. Concluded it was the Catholic college established by Dr Hughes — pleasantly situated fine building.[61]

7 May 1849 [Hart's first meditation]
Our very existence is in many ways a mystery to us, and a little reflection will show anyone the impossibility of explaining according to human ideas many things which we are bound to believe. And of these things some that are not usually called 'mysteries', e.g., the connexion of the soul with the body — death, heaven, hell; how it was that sin produced such lamentable effects in the world; how it was even that the Passion and Death of our B[lessed] Saviour effected the Redemption of the World — tho' this last is called a mystery.

In lesser matters, I may add the growth of plants and animals; their decay; disease; the apparent waste frequently witnessed in nature, the instinct of animals, etc. We can no doubt penetrate a short way into the causes of disease, of chemical change, of better or worse state of vegetation, etc. Such discoveries are frequently very useful and it is very desirable they should be made. But there is something still beyond our reach and it would almost seem that we are permitted to advance a certain distance in one direction, a certain distance in another, far enough to let us see that there are laws — at present to us mysteries — by which everything in this world is regulated.

We find ourselves then placed in the midst of mysteries, moral and physical, and at the same time we find that we are in some degree masters of our own actions, that is that we have 'free will'. In this world of mysteries it would be vain to hope to discover what course of conduct the Great Being who created us wishes us to pursue, if he did not reveal it to us himself. We are told on his authority (into the proofs that it *is his* authority I need not enter) that man was originally created a pure and elevated being, that by disobedience he fell and entailed the punishment of his sin on the whole race, that by this all men became corrupt — their tastes and passions depraved — that they became blind to their true interest and happiness.

That the great Creator, seeing the misery and blindness to which they were reduced, formed the merciful design of rescuing them; that God himself came down upon earth in the form of man and, after pointing out the way to please him and secure eternal happiness, endured severe torments and death and by so doing opened heaven to such of the human race as should deserve it by leading virtuous lives in accordance with the principles laid down by him. That before hc left this earth he instituted sacraments and means of grace, which tho' to human reason may seem trifling must not be judged by such criticism. The only question being did God command this to be done and does he attach importance to it?

In the same way it is wrong and absurd for anyone to say of any point of faith held by any sect or individual — 'it is absurd, I cannot understand it, how can it be'. The only question is has it been revealed by God. The query may suggest itself that, if God be all powerful and at the same time so merciful and anxious for the salvation of the human race, why does he not with one word blot out sin and its effects and make man good and happy as he was before — why did he allow him to fall[?] All these are mysteries which we cannot understand. We only know that things are so, that we are a fallen race, that our B. Saviour came on earth full of mercy and meekness, that he seems to have been fully aware of the [im]possibility of our seeing the reasons of all these things and that apparently on that account he bids us 'be as little children'; that is to come to one so mild and gentle and good with perfect confidence, to do implicitly what he desires, as children obey their parents without at all times knowing the reasons for what they do but feeling sure that it is for their good.

It seems to be his wish that we should regard him in this light as a kind father and affectionate friend, who, seeing the improbability of our knowing and doing what is right of ourselves, has undertaken to guide and save us. For this reason we should frequently consult him and prefer our requests to him by prayer, and he in many places commands us to do so. Viewing our Saviour in this light would seem, independently of the good effect on ourselves, to have a beneficial effect on our conduct and intercourse with others. Regarding them all as sons and daughters of the same kind parent, who takes the same tender interest in one that he does in another, we cannot fail of being more mild and charitable, upright in our dealings and above all careful not to be in any way the cause of sin to others, of provoking to offend him by anger, etc.

15 May . . . [*on avoiding vice, keeping 'before our minds that we are here in a temporary obscurity . . . detaching ourselves as much as possible from this world, which is as it were a shadow or cloud which will one day roll away and disappear and the true state of things will become apparent', c. 500 words*]

21 May

By this should not be understood that we are to neglect our affairs in this world. If we be farmers we are to mind our farms, if merchants our trade, if lawyers our law honestly and diligently — avoiding all injustice or anything forbidden by the law of God. It is the lot of man to labour and as long as he is left in this world, it is his duty to labour faithfully in the vocation to which God has appointed him. . .

24 May . . . [*while we are all weak creatures dependent on God, men prepare themselves for greatness, not by dreaming, but by a rigorous use of their faculties. 'The true way to act is to perform the duties which fall to one's lot with vigour and fidelity, avoiding all that may injure or weaken any of the*

mental or physical qualities, and taking advantage of all legitimate means
within our reach for their improvement. . . Ambition alone will not enable a
man to rise high.' c. 800 words]

Monday, 28 May
Since 5 May have been in N. York. On my arrival found JD not yet quite
settled in his office. In a few days however he got all finished, name up,
etc. Found Wm. Mitchel hard at work studying Law, fully determined
to commence in JD's office. On 12 May, I was sitting in JD's office when
in came E. W. [*recte* W. E.] Robinson with a most important face, saying
he had just got an appointment for Wm. M. — and that he should go
off to Washington that evening. At first I was sorry, as everything seemed
to be going so pleasantly, and with such a good prospect for JD and Wm.
M. But since see that it is better for Wm. M. and in the end may make
him a better lawyer, tho' at first it seemed as if it would distract his mind
and turn him from steady professional industry.

He went off [Sunday, 13 May]. Same day I dined with Dr H. Had
long chat with him. On Wednesday or Thursday MO'F returned to N.
York, JD having written for him as there were letters here for him. Had
spent pleasant time enough walking thro' country, etc. During this
time, I have generally gone down town every day to dine with JD, we
having discovered an excellent place (the Franklin) to dine about 2 p.m.
— and have walked somewhere from 4–6 p.m. or so with him.

During this time I have read: *Marion's Life* by [W. G.] Simms, 1 vol.[62],
Campaign Sketches of the War in Mexico under Gen. Taylor by [W. S.] Henry,
1 vol.; *Mexico* by Waddy Thompson, 1 vol.; *Statesmen of America in 1848*
by Mrs [Sarah Mytton] Maury, 1 vol.; *Washington and his Generals* by
Headly, 2 vols.; some mensuration; written letters, kept Journal, made
extracts, etc. . . [*reflecting on merits of physical training, regrets not avail-*
ing of local gymnasium the previous winter, c. 250 words]

It has also occurred to me that I might with advantage have been
learning something of chemistry, particularly agricultural, from Dr
Antisell during the winter. Must . . . be more careful to 'look out for
the Engine when the bull runs'; above all must give up habit of repining

over what can't be helped; or even talking about or expatiating on it, which is nearly as bad as repining and leads to it.

Have got every week letters, each giving a more favourable account of Pauline's health — and all stating Ady is remarkably [well] and little more. Have been waiting here for money to go somewhere thro' the country. But do not regret the delay as it has been a means of affording company to JD, who would otherwise have been very lonely since Mitchel, who was constantly with him and living in the same house, has left for Washington. Went once a few days after my return with JD to see Mrs B — to tell about Pauline's health. Have paid no other visits except one to Dr H. MO'F has (apparently finally) declared his intention of remaining in America.

Saturday, 9 June
On Tuesday wrote to Mr O'H[ara] about giving up deeds, having heard that he refused to do so by the previous mail; also wrote to lawyer.

Spent several days of the previous week and also several days of this one just past listening to important trial for murder, in which Mr C[harles] O'Conor and [David] Hoffman were engaged for prisoner. Admired ability with which CO'C conducted [case] and Hoffman's eloquence. Case was a striking lesson to dissipated people.

Yesterday for the first time saw Mighan,[63] of whose arrival I had heard. He has already set up a boarding [house] on a moderate scale and with good success, and I feel every confidence he will finally do well. Amused much by his remarks on the precocity of young chaps here and by his account of Poll's doings — her being sick, etc., at home. It seems curious to have Mighan out here, just as if the whole stock, lock and barrel was coming out. He seems to take a very sensible view of the advantages of this country, particularly for his children. We will do what we can for him as he is an honest fellow.

On Monday last mounted a white hat — *generally admitted to be very becoming.* Mighan tells me that I have got a regular Yankee look, which surprises me as I thought I looked quite like an Irishman. Yet it shows me, however, how unconsciously one slips as it were into a foreign appearance by living in a foreign country — even when you do not affect it but even rather avoid it as I have.

[*Extract from pensées*] Always trusting implicitly in the word of Divine Wisdom and Truth that the goods of this world are perishable and unworthy [of] the affections of an immortal being, we should at all times be ready to give away to any amount that may be necessary for the relief of distress, spread or sustainment of faith, religion and virtue. Do not at present see or think that the rigorous prosecution of business, even a lucrative one, and a moderate and unostentatious enjoyment of the goods and conveniences of life is incompatible with the above state of mind — provided one does not allow such affairs to absorb all one's thoughts and affections, and acts with strict honesty and integrity. . .

A good man should not reject wealth if thrown in his way, nor slacken in legitimate energy in the pursuit of his business if he sees that he is becoming wealthy. . . A great deal of good may be done by wealth well applied — tho' the reflection should be indulged in with great caution, as it is not infrequently used as a salve to the conscience when a man is really avariciously pursuing wealth . . . [*on resisting 'three great enemies': avarice, 'concupiscence of the flesh' and ambition, c. 600 words*]

14 June
It seems to be a duty to keep ourselves in good health, not so much in order that we may live long as that while we live we may have the full use of our faculties. . . One cannot discharge *any* duties even spiritual ones so well when in ill health . . . the real enjoyment which good health brings seems to be one of those innocent pleasures of this life, like the beauties of nature, etc., in which we may freely indulge, if with the indulgence are combined a continued *and grateful* recollection of the *Giver* — to whose goodness *alone* we owe it — and also a fraternal feeling and willingness to relieve those less favoured in this respect than ourselves . . .

Above all things we should most scrupulously avoid the great folly and wickedness of ridiculing any person who may be deformed or

afflicted with any chronic disease. It is wicked because most uncharitable and unkind, and foolish because it is ridiculing our own fallen
nature, liable perhaps at any moment to meet with a similar mis-
chance. Besides it is no merit of ours that we are not similarly
afflicted. Besides the time in which we shall each move about, the one
in his well-shaped the other in his deformed body, is but a moment
— and a few days in the grave will leave but little to choose between
them. In the next world, by all accounts, it is not *the 'cut' or colour of
the coat* but the manner of wearing it that they look to. . . [Mean-
while,] we must work our vessel cheerfully and contentedly, even if
it be frail or leaky, doing our best to repair and strengthen it as we go
along . . . [c. 200 words]

Sunday, 8 July
On board ship *Baltimore* for [Le] Havre: Got on 12th or 14th of June
letter telling me to prepare to leave America. Made every preparation
and enquiry and finally decided on coming to Havre in *Baltimore*, to sail
on 2 July from N. York. Took leave of different friends. Left America
with some feelings of regret. It is, I think, always natural to do so when
one has been even just pleasant in a place. However, tho' not knowing
very many persons, I had met with much kindness and had been continually gratified by the obvious prosperity of the country, the success
of its free institutions, and with many of the qualities of the people.
Also of course I left behind some very dear friends. However, I believe
I never left any place where I had been so long in better spirits for, after
all, the prevailing feeling was anxiety to see those at home again.

    I felt remarkably well — much the better as I conceived in mind and
body of my journey to America. I had also lost much if not all of that
weak feeling finding myself alone 'and on my own hook', to which I
was formerly subject, and on the whole I felt myself more a man of the
world. I felt however regret that I had not done a few things which it
would be desirable to have done — e.g., seen the West, Lowell, [Mass-
achusetts]; more of the surface even of the State of NY, as about Bing-
hampton, etc.; tried even for a few weeks' engineering; or, as Antisell

suggested to me a few days before I left, have spent some of the spring boarding at some farmer's learning the American mode of doing things, preparatory to farming myself, etc.

The simplest way to satisfy the mind, whether any or what of these desirable things was *possible*, seems to me to be to consider how the time was spent, and what were the reasons for so spending it at the different periods where decisions were made. I feel confident that all the time I had the fullest intention and wish to spend it to the best advantage; this however is nothing to boast of, tho' such is the fact, and I consequently did what I could by my own judgement and the advice of others. On the whole therefore I think the time was *in general* pretty well laid out, tho' of course I do not pretend that it was spent as it should, or that the most [or] anything of the sort was made of it within the prescribed limits or according to the plan struck out.

[*Reading 'God and I', reflects that 'attention to exteriors of religion . . . hearing Mass regularly, at least on Sundays, exactness in saying prayers morning and evening, a short daily meditation and examination [of conscience], going to Confession and Communion at regular and not very far apart periods' and spiritual reading form framework of a virtuous life . . . c. 250 words*]

Sunday, 15 July
On board *Baltimore*. Thinking how had not ascertained clearly the most important fact by which to decide on a future residence in the W[est of] I[reland] as a farmer, namely what was to be made of it and whether one could live by it as I would wish and my friends would wish me to live . . . [*regrets not obtaining accurate information about farming, before 'being suddenly required to return to Europe'. His procrastination reminds him 'of the surpassing importance of attaining that state of mind in which we should wish to appear before God' . . . c. 850 words*]

20 October, 2 November [1849], 4 April 1850
The union of contemplative and active habits construct the most useful and perfect character. . . A man unaccustomed to speculation is confined to a narrow routine of action; a man of mere speculation

constructs visionary theories which have no practical utility . . . [*on study and business, c. 900 words*]

Saturday, 8 December 1849

13 Upper Merrion St., Dublin.[64] Have thought it well in recommencing to keep a sort of journal to give a sketch of the period from the time I left off writing one to the present time. The cabin passengers on board with me on the voyage from N. York to Havre were French people, two ladies and three gentlemen: A French merchant and his wife from N[ew] Orleans going home to Côteret, his native place where he had a *Terre*, to spend some time for health, etc. An elderly French lady from Savannah, a young French mercantile man; and a peculiar, rather nice looking old Frenchman from Central America, who had lost his voice and spoke in whispers and was going home to get good medical advice.

He was lame from a wound received in the Mexican War of Independence in which he had fought. On one occasion he said he had escaped (when he would otherwise have shortly been shot) by making a sign of freemasonry which was understood by the Spanish officer.

Notes to Introduction

(The National Library of Ireland is abbreviated to NLI and Trinity College, Dublin, to TCD)

1   Quoted in Gerard J. Lyne, *The Lansdowne Estate in Kerry under W. S. Trench, 1849–72* (Dublin, 2001), p. 101.

2   Cormac Ó Gráda, *Black '47 and Beyond: The Great Irish Famine in History, Economy and Memory* (Princeton University Press, 1999), p. 114; Edward O'Donnell, '"The Scattered Debris of the Irish Nation": The Famine Irish and New York City, 1845–55', in E. Margaret Crawford (ed.), *The Hungry Stream: Essays on Emigration and Famine* (Belfast, 1997), pp. 52–3.

3   Hart family Bible in the possession of Professor John M. Dillon; F. S. L. Lyons, *John Dillon: A Biography* (London, 1868), p. 6. I am indebted to Mr Fergus Redmond, Rathcoole, County Dublin, for help in locating Hart's grave in the old churchyard of Kilmacktolway, the inscription over which reads: 'This is the burial place of the Harts of Greenogue.'

4   Patrick O'Donoghue, CM, Castleknock College, Dublin, 18 May 2000, to editor; TCD, Dillon Papers, MS 6463.

5   Brendan Ó Cathaoir, *John Blake Dillon: Young Irelander* (Dublin, 1990), pp. 47–51.

6   Charles Gavan Duffy, *Four Years of Irish History, 1845–1849* (London, 1883), p. 609.

7   *Nation*, 27 May 1848; Ó Cathaoir, *Dillon*, pp. 50–1, 79.

8   Dillon to Adelaide, 30 August 1848: TCD, Dillon Papers, MS 6455/68; *Annual Register*, 1848 (Chronicle), p. 94.

9   Duffy, *Four Years*, p. 525; Miss Ghee to Duffy [undated]: NLI, Duffy Papers, MS 8005/48; Ó Cathaoir, *Dillon*, p. 101.

10 Henry David Thoreau, *Walden and Civil Disobedience* (first published 1849; New York, 1983 edn.), p. 390.

11 Michael Doheny, *The Felon's Track*, ed. Arthur Griffith (Dublin, 1914 edn.), pp. 184, 206.

12 Robert Sloan, *William Smith O'Brien and the Young Ireland Rebellion of 1848* (Dublin, 2000), p. 294.

13 Sloan, *O'Brien*, p. 290.

14 MacManus narrative: NLI, Duffy Papers, MS 5886; Sloan, *O'Brien*, pp. 277–8.

15 Kavanagh narrative: NLI, Duffy Papers, MS 5886. Statement identified by initials 'JK'. President of the Fitzgerald club in Dublin, Kavanagh would serve under Meagher during the American Civil War and die at the battle of Antietam in 1862, aged thirty-six: Doheny, *Felon's Track*, pp. 303–4; T. F. O'Sullivan, *The Young Irelanders* (Tralee, 1944), p. 375.

16 Ó Cathaoir, *Dillon*, p. 87.

17 Daunt journal: NLI, MS 3040. Entry for 28 July 1848, the date Hart's diary opens. Daunt, too, wrote some time after the events described.

18 MacManus narrative.

19 Ó Cathaoir, *Dillon*, 105.

20 *New York Daily Tribune*, 16, 17 October 1848.

21 Ó Cathaoir, 'American Fenianism and Canada, 1865–71' in *Irish Sword*, viii (1967), pp. 77–87; *Irish Times*, 30 December 1998.

22 *Dictionary of American History* (5 vols, New York, 1951), i, pp. 297–301; David A. Wilson, *United Irishmen, United States* (Dublin,1998), p. 84.

23 Hereward Senior, *The Fenians and Canada* (Toronto, 1978), p. 29.

24 *Ibid.*, pp. 30–1.

25 William D'Arcy, *The Fenian Movement in the United States, 1858–86* (New York, 1947), p. 5; Senior, *Fenians and Canada*, pp. 27, 31–2. Edward Alexander Theller: Ardent foe of British presence in North America who never forsook the Irish cause; b. Coleraine 1804, emigrated to Lower Canada (Quebec) 1826, settled in Detroit 1836; after the abortive rebellion of 1837 in Upper and Lower Canada, assisted Canadian refugees and American sympathisers to invade the two provinces; issued a revolutionary appeal to Irish and French Canadian inhabitants of Upper Canada (Ontario); arrested, found guilty of treason, death sentence commuted to transportation to New South Wales; escaped from Quebec jail to hero's welcome in US; settled in Rochester, New York, where he became secretary of the local branch of the Repeal Association; enjoined members to proclaim themselves 'the enemies of slavery in every form and in every clime, and the friends of the oppressed of every creed and colour'; d. California 1859: *Dictionary of Canadian Biography* (Toronto, 1985) VIII. Samuel May, Boston, 19 Sept. 1848, to Mary Carpenter: Clare Taylor, *British and American Abolitionists* (Edinburgh, 1974), p. 328.

26 Ignatius Murphy, *The Diocese of Killaloe, 1800–1850* (Dublin, 1992), pp. 205–7, on O'Gorman's escape; Michael Glazier (ed.), *The Encyclopedia of the Irish in America* (Notre Dame, 1999), p. 727; Doheny to Smith O'Brien, 20 August 1858: NLI, O'Brien Papers, MS 446/3058; O'Gorman narrative: NLI, Duffy Papers, MS 5886; Desmond Ryan, *The Fenian Chief: A Biography of James Stephens* (Dublin, 1967), p. 360; O'Gorman to Hart, 3 December 1888: TCD, Dillon Papers, MS 6457/492.

27 *Thom's Directory* (Dublin, 1850 edn.); Ó Cathaoir, 'Smith O'Brien's Retribution' in *North Munster Antiquarian Journal*, xxvii (1985), pp. 70–4; O'Flaherty to O'Brien, 18 July 1857: NLI, O'Brien Papers, MS 445/2966; *Galway Vindicator*, 1 April 1857.

28 Ó Cathaoir, *Dillon*, p. 126; the graves of John and William Mitchel are in the Unitarian cemetery, Newry.

29 J. J. St Mark, 'Matilda and William Tone in New York and Washington after 1798' in *Éire-Ireland*, xxii, no. 4 (winter 1987), pp. 4–10.

30   T. W. Moody, R. B. McDowell and C. J. Woods (eds.), *The Writings of Theobald
     Wolfe Tone, 1763–98* (Oxford, 2001), ii, p. 326.

31   'Joseph Brenan' by Michael Cavanagh: NLI, MS 3225, p. 38; Ryan, *Fenian Chief*,
     p. 364; John Mitchel, *Jail Journal* (Dublin, 1913 edn.), pp. 287, 405, 447.

32   *United Irishman* (Dublin), 12 February 1848; *People* (New York), 14 April 1849.

33   Adelaide Dillon memoir: TCD, Dillon Papers, MS 6457e.

34   TCD, Dillon Papers, MS 6465.

35   Adelaide Dillon, Dublin, to John Blake Dillon, 15 May 1849: TCD, Dillon
     Papers, MS 6455/106.

36   *King's Inns Admission Papers, 1607–1867* (Dublin, 1982).

37   John O'Hagan, Florence, to Adelaide Dillon, 11 June 1856: TCD, Dillon Papers,
     MS 6456/324; TCD, Dillon Papers, MSS 6903/1, 19; Charles Hart, Pau, to
     William O'Hara, 7 June 1855: TCD, Dillon Papers, MS 6455/295.

38   Duffy, *My Life in Two Hemispheres* (2 vols, London, 1898), i, p. 265.

39   Máirtín Ó Murchú, Dublin Institute for Advanced Studies, 14 December 1999,
     to editor; Ó Murchú, *Cumann Buan-Choimeádta na Gaeilge: Tús an Athréimnithe*
     (Baile Átha Cliath, 2001), pp. 217–18; Lyons, *Dillon*, p. 20.

40   Pauline Hart died in 1850, aged 20: Ó Cathaoir, *Dillon*, p. 122; Charles Hart,
     Castle Rock, to John Dillon, 7 June 1886: TCD, Dillon Papers, MS 6903/8a.

41   Hart to Dillon, 9 June 1886: TCD Dillon Papers, MS 6903/8b. The Marquis of
     Hartington (later Duke of Devonshire) broke with Gladstone over Home Rule
     and, as leader of the Liberal Unionists, maintained Salisbury's Conservatives in
     power until 1892; Joseph Chamberlain (1836–1914) and George (later 1st Vis-
     count) Goschen were other leading Liberal Unionists.

42   Hart, Dublin, to Anne Deane, Ballaghaderreen, 6 December 1890: TCD, Dillon
     Papers, MS 6891/31. Deane was a niece of John Blake Dillon, who 'looked on
     his children as her own': Sophia O'Brien, 'Mrs Deane of Ballaghaderreen' in *Irish
     Monthly*, July 1937, p. 477.

43   John Dillon to Hart, 2 January 1891: TCD, Dillon Papers, MS 6905/36; Lyons,
     Dillon, p. 113. Arthur Balfour was a Conservative politician who, as Chief Sec-
     retary for Ireland, 1887–91, earned the epithet 'Bloody Balfour'.

44   Hart to John Dillon, 13 May 1889: TCD, Dillon Papers, MS 6903/7; William
     Dillon to Hart, 20 May 1889: TCD, Dillon Papers, MS 6904/5.

45   William Dillon to Hart, 12 October 1888: TCD, Dillon Papers, MS 6904/2; J.
     W. Cummings, Denver, to William Dillon, 23 July 1890; H. J. McDevitt to Dil-
     lon, 20 September 1890; Dillon to Hart, 21 September 1890: TCD, Dillon
     Papers, MSS 6904/12, 14.

46   Hart to John Dillon, 8 April 1898: TCD, Dillon Papers, MS 6905/74; Charles
     O'Connor, QC, 28 May 1898: TCD, Dillon Papers, MSS 6905/37, 46.

47 Hart to Dillon, 8 April, 16 May 1898: TCD, Dillon Papers, MSS 6905/74, 76, 77; Dillon to Hart, 26 August [1893?]: TCD, Dillon Papers, MS 6903/87.

48 Elizabeth Dillon diary, 11 July 1898: TCD, Dillon Papers, MS 6700.

49 *Weekly Freeman*, 15 October 1898.

50 Hart had been trustee of a marriage settlement between John Joseph Mahon and Augusta M. M. Alen; the plaintiffs named in the High Court writ were Luke Alen Mahon, his son Randal, and Gertrude Buckley, of Dublin: TCD, Dillon Papers, MSS 6905/37, 47; Elizabeth Dillon diary, MS 6701; *Irish Times*, 18 October 1898.

51 The letters cited are: TCD, Dillon Papers, MSS 6903/106/92/100; Wilfrid Scawen Blunt, *The Land War in Ireland* (London, 1912), pp. 324, 364, 444; *A Portrait of the Artist as a Young Man* (Harmondsworth, 1960 edn.), p. 59.

52 M. J. Crean, Limerick, to Dillon, 17 October 1898: TCD, Dillon Papers, MS 6903/100.

53 I am indebted to Professor Ó Murchú for the text of the resolution. See also *Weekly Nation Supplement*, 29 October 1898; letter from SPIL secretary: TCD, Dillon Papers, MS 6903/108.

Notes to Narrative

1 When the police raided Druid Lodge searching for her brother-in-law, Pauline Hart asked to see an arrest warrant: Ó Cathaoir, *Dillon*, p. 92; *Thom's Directory* (Dublin, 1850 edn.).

2 While admiring Thomas Telford's suspension bridge, Hart confused the locomotive inventor, George Stephenson, who died on 12 August 1848, with his son, Robert, who built many long-span railway bridges, most notably the Britannia Bridge over the Menai Strait.

3 The Liverpool authorities wanted the Habeas Corpus Suspension Bill extended to their city, where, due to the Famine influx, Irish Catholics numbered 100,000 out of a population of 375,000, and magistrates claimed Confederate clubs could arm two to four thousand men: Ó Cathaoir, *Dillon*, 78; John Saville, *1848: The British State and the Chartist Movement* (London, 1987), pp. 152–6.

4 Smith O'Brien was arrested at Thurles railway station on 5 August 1848.

5 Benedict Arnold was an American general who conspired to betray West Point to the British during the Revolution. The capture of John André (see note 10) gave him time to escape: *Dictionary of American History*.

6 John O'Hagan, *Nation* contributor, Irish Confederation council member; later lecturer in political economy at Newman's University, appointed judge. Like Hart

and John Edward Pigot (note 24), O'Hagan was essentially a cultural nationalist who did not take part in rising: *Nation*, 24 June 1848; Ó Cathaoir, *Dillon*, pp. 74–5, 132, 142.

7   Dickens wrote of Boston: 'I almost believed the whole affair could be taken up piecemeal like a child's toy and crammed into a little box': Charles Dickens, *American Notes* (London, 1842), p. 15.

8   In 1775 the American militia besieging Boston sent 1,200 men to seize Bunker Hill, but they built a redoubt on Breed's Hill instead. Although overwhelmed by British forces, Bunker Hill was regarded as a moral victory. General Joseph Warren fell there: *Dictionary of American History*.

9   Charles O'Conor, Irish-American lawyer, son of United Irishman: Ó Cathaoir, *Dillon*, p. 75.

10 John André, adjutant general of British army in North America, captured by three American irregulars, convicted of spying and hanged in 1780: *Dictionary of American History*.

11 Hart uses 'gentlemany', an obsolete form of 'gentlemanly', throughout his narrative.

12 John Caldwell Calhoun (1782–1850), US statesman and political philosopher, born of Scots-Irish parents on South Carolina frontier: *The Oxford Companion to American History* (New York, 1966).

13 Marie Joseph Lafayette, French soldier who fought with American colonists, friend of George Washington: *Ibid*.

14 Thaddeus Kosciusko, Polish soldier who fought with Americans: *Chambers Biographical Dictionary* (Edinburgh, 1997).

15 Susan and Edward Bill, New York friends who provided conduit for the Hart/Dillon correspondence: Ó Cathaoir, *Dillon*, p. 102; Mrs H was probably wife of unidentified Dr H.

16 Initial reports raised the hopes of Hart and his friends. On 12 September 1848 about 300 insurgents attacked Portlaw constabulary barracks in County Waterford. The attack failed when one rebel was shot dead and two others were wounded: Brendan Kiely, *The Waterford Rebels of 1849* (Dublin, 1999), p. 36.

17 Lewis Cass served as major general in the War of 1812. Democratic presidential nominee in 1848 against victorious Whig candidate, Zachary Taylor: Lawrence Phillips, *Dictionary of Biographical Reference* (London, 1871).

18 Winfield Scott, US general who distinguished himself at battle of Lundy's Lane (1814) and during war against Mexico, 1846–8: *Chambers*, p. 1,663.

19 James Cantwell (1818–75), Dublin mercantile assistant, Irish Confederation council member. Later Fenian agent in Paris, Dublin hotel proprietor: Doheny, *Felon's Track*, p. 303; D'Arcy, *Fenian Movement in United States*, p. 13n.

20 During the Tipperary rising Dillon confronted a troop of cavalry at a barricade in Killenaule: Ó Cathaoir, *Dillon*, pp. 84–5.

21   Maurice Richard Leyne (1820–54), kinsman of O'Connell. As in the case of
      Duffy, the government failed to convict him. On revival of the *Nation* in 1849,
      Leyne joined Duffy in editing it: Gary Owens (ed.), 'Patrick O'Donohue's nar-
      rative of the 1848 rising' in *Tipperary Historical Journal* (1998), p. 45; Doheny,
      Felon's Track, p. 308.

22   P. J. Barry, Dublin law clerk; secretary of Grattan club, of which Meagher was
      president; 'loud and vainglorious' and suspected of having 'occult relations with
      the police': Duffy, *Four Years*, p. 673.

23   John Mackey, parish priest of Clonoulty, interceded with Dublin Castle on behalf
      of rebels; Gore Jones, resident magistrate, after O'Brien's arrest passed on his
      request to have a portmanteau collected from Doheny's home in Cashel: NLI,
      O'Brien Papers, MS 8657; Owens (ed.), 'O'Donohue's narrative', p. 42.

24   John Edward Pigot, eldest son of Chief Baron David Richard Pigot and *Nation*
      contributor. 'With O'Curry and O'Donovan and Petrie he descended into the
      neglected fields of Irish literature and formed societies . . . to rescue from obliv-
      ion our ancient manuscripts': obituary, *Nation*, 8 July 1871.

25   William Walsh, b. Waterford 1804; Catholic bishop of Halifax, Nova Scotia,
      1845: *Dictionary of Canadian Biography*.

26   John Joseph Hughes, b. County Tyrone 1797; first Catholic archbishop of New
      York 1850: *Encyclopedia of Irish in America*, pp. 394–5, 680.

27   John Hetherington Drumm, medical student and *Nation* sub-editor; vice-presi-
      dent of St Patrick's club along with William Mitchel and Thomas Devin Reilly
      (John Mitchel was president); lectured on Irish antiquities, became Methodist
      clergyman: *Nation*, 3 June 1848; *United Irishman*, 4 March 1848; Doheny, *Felon's
      Track*, p. 300.

28   Richard O'Gorman was accompanied by John O'Donnell and Daniel Doyle, Lim-
      erick solicitors: O'Sullivan, *The Young Irelanders*, pp. 358–9.

29   Richard Stockton Emmet (1821–97), grandson of Thomas Addis Emmet, the
      brother of Robert Emmet executed in 1803: T. A. Emmet, *The Emmet Family*
      (New York, 1898), p. 256.

30   William James MacNeven, son of William MacNeven who had been on the
      United Irish Directory with Thomas Addis Emmet: *Encyclopedia of Irish in Amer-
      ica*, p. 679.

31   John McClenahan, edited *Limerick Reporter*; in New York involved with Reilly's
      People and John Mitchel's *Citizen: Jail Journal*, p. 443.

32   Thomas Antisell after the insurrection escaped to the US, where he became a sci-
      entist: *Ibid*.

33   Patrick James Smyth (1826–85), educated with Meagher at Clongowes Wood Col-
      lege, County Kildare. After the rising fled to the US in the same vessel as Dillon;
      helped Mitchel to escape from Tasmanian penal settlement; later Home Rule MP

for Westmeath and Tipperary, but according to Parnell joined a conservative clerical clique: Robert Kee, *The Laurel and Ivy . . . Charles Stewart Parnell and Irish Nationalism* (London, 1993), p. 90; *Jail Journal*, pp. 448–9; Ó Cathoir, *Dillon*, p. 100.

34 McGee's criticism of the Catholic church for its authoritarianism and hostility to republicanism brought him into conflict with Bishop Hughes. He later modified his political views, growing increasingly pro-clerical and anti-revolutionary. In 1857 he moved to Montreal at the invitation of the Irish community there. Elected to Dominion parliament 1867, denounced Fenianism, assassinated by Fenian sympathizer 1868: *Encyclopedia of Irish in America*, p. 582; Ryan, *Fenian Chief*, pp. 353–4.

35 Orestes Brownson, Yankee convert to Catholicism and religious fanatic: Ó Cathaoir, *Dillon*, pp. 113–14. Dillon was equally censorious of Doheny's behaviour.

36 John Caldwell (1769–1850), b. near Ballymoney, County Antrim, son of a Presbyterian farmer and linen manufacturer. His brother Richard (see Introduction) organized rebel forces in north Antrim in 1798. When the rising was suppressed, John was imprisoned and Richard sentenced to death. Their father's intercession with Lord Cornwallis (note 38) secured their release on condition the family went into exile: Kerby Miller in *Encyclopedia of the Irish in America*, pp. 95–6.

37 Daniel Webster (1782–1852), American lawyer and statesman.

38 Charles Cornwallis, British general who surrendered to Washington at Yorktown in 1781. On arrival in Ireland as Lord Lieutenant in the aftermath of the 1798 insurrection, he was shocked by the military licence: Marianne Elliott, *The Catholics of Ulster: A History* (London, 2000), p. 260.

39 John Charles Frémont (1813–90), US explorer in the news because he had been dismissed from the army for controversial activities in California: *American National Biography*.

40 Dillon read John Milner's *End of Religious Controversy* while hiding on the Aran Islands before escaping to US dressed as a priest: Ó Cathaoir, *Dillon*, pp. 95, 100.

41 Hart was reminded of John Gray (1816–75), proprietor-editor of *Freeman's Journal*: Henry Boylan, *A Dictionary of Irish Biography* (Dublin, 1998).

42 John Macpherson Berrien is here compared to John Kenyon (1812–69), the fire-eating parish priest of Templederry, County Tipperary.

43 Nicholas Ball (1791–1865), Irish judge.

44 George Catlin's 470 pictures illustrating the life and customs of Native Americans are now in the National Museum, Washington.

45 D. H. Mahan, mathematician and writer.

46 Henry O'Hara, recorder of Galway: *Thom's Directory* (Dublin, 1850 edn).

47 George Washington's former home and burial place.

48 When Zachary Taylor died in 1850, Millard Fillmore succeeded him as the thirteenth US president.

49 Whitley Stokes (1763–1845), fellow of TCD and early member of Dublin Society of United Irishmen: *DNB*. Tone regarded Stokes 'as the *very best* man I have ever known': Moody, McDowell and Woods, *Writings of Tone*, ii, p. 293.

50 Lucien (1775–1840) and Jerome (1784–1860) Bonaparte, brothers of Napoleon.

51 Patrick MacDermott (d. 1812), priest, kept a boarding school at Collège des Irlandais. After becoming king of Westphalia in 1807, Jerome bestowed an annual pension on MacDermott: Liam Swords, *The Green Cockade: The Irish in the French Revolution* (Dublin, 1989), pp. 140–1.

52 Mrs Tone must have been thinking of the Music Hall, Fishamble Street, where Kane O'Hara was vice-president of the Musical Academy. He was described as long-winded and 'having the appearance of an old fop . . . the very pink of gentility': J. T. Gilbert, *History of the City of Dublin* (3 vols., Dublin, 1859), i, p. 79, iii, p. 269.

53 William Witherington, Grafton Street, woollen draper and wine merchant: *DNB*.

54 Edward Fanning, rector, Banagher, County Londonderry, 1751–91.

55 Sir Lucius O'Brien, William Smith O'Brien's grandfather.

56 The Basilica of the Assumption of the Virgin Mary in Baltimore was the first Roman Catholic cathedral built in the US.

57 This is the first passage in section II, which Hart wrote at the back of his journal. It has been integrated into the main text.

58 The article was entitled 'The Sicilian Style', not 'Fashion': *People*, 14 April 1849.

59 Thomas Addis Emmet (1828–1919), physician and writer, grandson of United Irishman Thomas Addis Emmet: Glazier (ed.), *Encyclopedia of the Irish in America*.

60 Ira Harris, chief justice of New York State.

61 In 1841 Bishop Hughes invited the Jesuits to take over St John's College, later Fordham University: Glazier (ed.), *Encyclopedia of Irish in America*, p. 680. I am indebted to Caoimhín Micheál, New York and Dingle, County Kerry, for identifying the college.

62 Francis Marion, American revolutionary general.

63 Mighan must have been a servant who emigrated because Druid Lodge was let for the summer of 1849: Adelaide to Hart, 1 June 1849, TCD, Dillon Papers, MS 6455/113.

64 13 Upper Merrion Street was where William O'Hara practised as a solicitor: *Thom's Directory* (Dublin,1850 edn.). The 'sort of journal' has not survived.

Bibliography

American National Biography (New York, 1999)

Chambers Biographical Dictionary (Edinburgh, 6th edn., 1997)

Duffy, Charles Gavan, *Four Years of Irish History, 1845–1849* (London, 1883)

Glazier, Michael (ed.), *The Encyclopedia of the Irish in America* (Notre Dame, 1999)

Lyons, F. S. L., *John Dillon: A Biography* (London, 1968)

Mitchel, John, *Jail Journal* (Dublin, 1913 edn.)

Moody, T. W., MacDowell, R. B. and Woods, C. J. (eds.), *The Writings of Theobald Wolfe Tone, 1763–98*; vol. II: *America, France and Bantry Bay, August 1795 to December 1796* (Oxford, 2001)

Ó Cathaoir, Brendan, *John Blake Dillon: Young Irelander* (Dublin, 1990)

Senior, Hereward, *The Fenians and Canada* (Toronto, 1978)

Sloan, Robert, *William Smith O'Brien and the Young Ireland Rebellion of 1848* (Dublin, 2000)

Wilson, David A., *United Irishmen, United States: Immigrant Radicals in the Early Republic* (Dublin, 1998)

Index